NOTICE & WONDER

Matt —
Thank you so much
for your support!

— Mark J.

NOTICE & WONDER:

A GUIDE TO CREATING MEANINGFUL FEEDBACK CONVERSATIONS THAT HAVE A LASTING IMPACT

MARK JOY

NEW DEGREE PRESS

NOTICE & WONDER:

A Guide to Creating Meaningful Feedback Conversations That Have a Lasting Impact

ISBN   978-1-63730-721-2   *Paperback*

           978-1-63730-858-5   *Kindle Ebook*

           978-1-63730-989-6   *Ebook*

CONTENTS

INTRODUCTION

FEEDBACK AS OUR FRIEND

A few years back I came across a TEDx Talk focused on inclusive design that had an exciting twist. Mara Mintzer, who gave the talk, is an expert in child-friendly cities. The United Nations Children's Fund (UNICEF) outlines on its website that a child-friendly city is "a city, town or community in which the voices, needs, priorities and rights of children are an integral part of public policies, programmes and decisions." Mara is also the director of an organization called Growing Up Boulder (GUB). For designing public spaces in Boulder, Colorado, she shared that she and her team enlist the help of the often-overlooked experts: children.

I sat down with Mara to learn more about GUB and its work. From idea brainstorming to implementation, GUB approaches its projects and works with children as true partners and collaborators. First, Mara and her team visit the children in their classrooms. Then, they connect the children with city planning experts to iterate the feasibility of their ideas. Later, the primary school-aged children would present their final ideas to city officials and discuss their work and why they went in the directions they did. I found this fascinating because during our conversation Mara expressed that this approach challenged children to carefully reflect on what changes they wanted to see in their city. It also pushed the adults to think differently and be challenged in their own thinking.

For many people getting feedback from kids could almost feel frivolous. But Mara and GUB realized how to act on the input and ideas from the children, and her team's public space designs exponentially improved. I wondered if all of us could learn from this to make feedback our friend, no matter who it comes from, and what I have found has transformed the way I see feedback today.

FEEDBACK & BULLYING

Feedback can come in multiple versions, both formally and informally, and our responses to it vary. David Bradford and Carole Robin outlined in their March 2021 *Thrive Global* article that we constantly receive feedback, and it's clear that this information is crucial for growth and learning. However, as documented in a 1996 *Psychological Bulletin* article by Avraham Kluger and Angelo DeNisi, why is it that—if we see feedback as necessary—feedback is rarely successful or effective? Seeing feedback as ineffective only appears to have worsened in the cyber world, with associated stress, according to Therese Huston's January 2021 *Harvard Business Review* piece, and a bias toward negativity, as noted by Braund et al. in their 2019 *Anxiety, Stress, and Coping* research article. So, even when we receive positive feedback, it's criticism and unfavorable feedback we dwell on most often because, psychologically, we have a bias or tendency to be pulled toward criticism.

A 2016 *PLOS ONE* research article by Kätsyri et al. showed that this negativity bias in the cyber world is associated with what we are more focused on in our social media newsfeeds. What might contribute to this is the fact that social media platforms amplify the posts that receive the most engagement, good or bad. Moreover, according to Nazir Hawi and Maya Samaha Rupert in their 2016 *Social Science Computer Review* article, identity and self-esteem connect to the presence on social media. They also note that when we consider two of the characteristics that make feedback effective, timeliness and personalization, the consequences of charged, in-the-moment, and personalized social media comments and reactions—cyberbullying—only intensifies this focus on the negative. This reminds me of something that Mara has learned to prioritize in her work with children: the need to build a space where the young people feel empowered, not bullied.

The skewing toward negativity in the age of information overload makes me think about why—for a while—receiving feedback was so difficult for me. It put me in this space of feeling like I was being bullied again, similar to when I was a teenager. It set off a fight-or-flight response within me, a familiar reaction that frequently surfaced in my first job at age sixteen.

What comes to mind when you think of bullying? For many, we may associate it with youth and our time in school. According to a July 2019 National Center for Education Statistics report written by Melissa Seldin and Christina Yanez, roughly 20 percent of students reported being bullied in school. Moreover, about 40 percent of students who reported being bullied thought that it would happen again. To press the issue further, a 2002 study published in the *Scandinavian*

Journal of Psychology by Eva Gemzøe Mikkelsen and Ståle Einarsen found that adult bullying is an extension of school and childhood behavior. Unfortunately, the issue of bullying doesn't go away just because we get older.

In Denise Salin's 2003 *Human Relations* journal article, Salin defines bullying as "repeated and persistent negative acts toward one or more individuals, which involve a perceived power imbalance and creates a hostile work environment." That said, how does bullying come about in the workplace? The foundation on which bullying can occur is what Salin calls enabling structures. Salin argued that "enabling structures and processes include conditions that make it possible for bullying to occur in the first place, which consist of a perceived power imbalance, low perceived costs, and dissatisfaction and frustration." A perceived power imbalance refers to the notion that the ones on the receiving end of the bullying, the victims or targets, feel inferior and powerless in attempting to defend themselves.

In my experience of overcoming workplace bullying, I found I had learned more about myself and about resilience than I gave myself credit for at the time. I even realized that feedback is essential and effective when taken as resilient feedback instead of bullied feedback. Bullied feedback takes the enabling structures of feedback at face value. It shows me that insufficient attention is paid to the enabling structures around delivering feedback effectively.

Perhaps feedback effectiveness falls short because the act of receiving feedback may take on some of the traits of bullying defined above. That's not to say that the feedback giver's intention is disingenuous or that the receiver is hypersensitive. Instead, it situates both the giver and receiver in taking a familiar approach when navigating the feedback conversations.

We'll talk more about this in the following chapters, but it's worth stressing that taking the "familiar approach" focuses on logical and more limited feedback navigation.

RESILIENT-BASED FEEDBACK

Too often, I have gone into a feedback conversation with colleagues or loved ones where, even though I knew we were entering the space with the best intentions, I found myself drowning in the *what-ifs* or worst-case scenarios in the lead-up to the conversation. Because of that I would resort to a "familiar" or "default" mode when partaking in those discussions, consisting of me being hyperaware of other's feelings and making sure that any feedback I provided didn't set off feelings associated with being bullied. As a result, when receiving feedback, I would automatically have that pit in my stomach, which reduced my ability to fully engage in genuine and intense listening. I was simply waiting for the negative critique or even an attack on my personal character to begin.

In contrast, feedback that is resilient-based surfaces assumptions and conditions generated by enabling feedback structures. Resilient-based feedback takes these structures and conditions as constantly changing and adapting. Because of this, resilient-based feedback assumes an intentional separation of the different types of feedback and a degree of flexibility in approach to moving through feedback conversations. Resilience is a process that speaks to the ability to learn from the past so that you can continuously adapt and increase your ability to stretch your boundaries of creative possibilities.

Mara's Growing Up Boulder success stories are rooted in resilient feedback. As a city councilperson or urban planning expert, the opportunity to work with children on designing public spaces allows listening and feedback cycles to unfold naturally. This expands the adults' boundaries of possibility and adaptability. This also brings about a space where the children feel intellectually safe to take their ideas in any direction. By the end of a project, they're able to see that their contributions to the effort were valued.

WHY THIS BOOK?

Feedback is a fickle thing mainly because without naming and examining the feedback structures it runs the risk of either compromising some aspect of psychological, emotional, social, or intellectual safety, or leaves us questioning the value of our input or output. However, for both the feedback giver and receiver, a resilient feedback approach reduces these potential worries and holds all parties accountable. This forms a bridge between feedback intent and action, which is the precise foundation on which *Notice & Wonder* builds.

I'm motivated to write this book because of what I've learned about resilience and its connections with what being bullied felt like and what feedback can sometimes feel like. After my experience with bullying, as I continued to navigate challenging or new workplaces or academic settings, I found connections between moments of feeling bullied and moments of engaging in feedback. I'm compelled to name these links in the following chapters of this book.

I observed these links most clearly in three experiences. The first when I transferred colleges at the end of my sophomore year. I didn't anticipate switching schools being as difficult as it was. However, I built on what I learned through my first job and was in control of how this transition would go. I could either spend all my time in my dorm room while slowly watching my grades and my self-esteem slip, or I could begin exploring how I made it work at my former school and surface themes and patterns that I could build on at this new school.

Second, when I started grad school I had a friend who insisted that I join a pop-up community choir that commemorates the legacy of Dr. Martin Luther King Jr. Little did I know I would continue to join that choir every year following until the COVID-19 pandemic forced us into quarantine for all of 2020, extending into 2021. I quickly realized that resilience thrives when paired with a sense of community and belonging, and for me that choir was it. There's something about the choir space that made me keep going back to it. I recently figured out what it was—I'd been able to be open and trusting in a way that I only dreamed of while working at that restaurant in high school.

Third and finally, as I went through my graduate student experience in the field of conflict resolution I realized that a common thread throughout was an emphasis on exploring enabling structures of conflict to varying degrees; structures that created or upheld power asymmetries, discord, or fueled division within systems, communities, or individuals. This speaks to the structural emphasis that I aim to place on feedback. Feedback isn't just content or context—it's both, and then some. This experience helped me understand that I need the trees to see the forest and the forest to see the trees.

To recap, resilient-based feedback works to decrease the feeling of being bullied by feedback and leverages a framework for resilient collaboration and community. A resilient-based approach to feedback stretches boundaries of creative possibility and strengthens the ability to adapt.

This book will explore resilient-based feedback as a method rooted in: Expansive thinking and creativity, Persistent conversation, Inclusion, and Compassionate listening. In short, the following pages are going to argue that resilient-based feedback is an E.P.I.C. process.

The following pages can be seen as a practical resource when navigating formal and informal feedback. This guide can be used by students in the classroom looking to broaden their support system, professionals early into their career wanting to leverage their network while building their resilient-based feedback muscles, or educators and managers who are looking to adopt a vision-oriented approach to engaging feedback.

Notice & Wonder gives readers a chance to see formal and informal feedback uncovered and how feedback may have stuck with you in your own life. This book will help you:

- Explore the neurological and psychological reactions associated with engaging feedback. Why do we respond in certain moments of feedback with a fight-or-flight response, while in other moments or spaces we're able to react with expansive thinking and creativity?
- Build awareness around your capacity to expand your boundaries of feedback possibilities. What does resilient-based feedback say about miscommunication, misinterpretation, community, and accountability?
- Acquire insights into how to engage in resilient feedback practices as a student, someone early in their career, or an educator or manager.

PART ONE

PART ONE

CHAPTER ONE:

FEEDBACK EFFECTIVENESS

———

DON'T FORGET TO FLOSS

I dread going to the dentist. Whenever I'm close to a checkup I get in my head about what the dentist might say about my teeth. So, I start flossing more as the appointment draws nearer, thinking I'll be able to convince Dr. J that I floss more often than I actually do.

I go into my appointment stressed about the possibility of having a cavity or something that would require me being in the dental chair, under that bright, shining light with the sound of dental tools humming in my ears, for any longer than necessary. "What if they find something serious? What if I need a filling or—even worse—another root canal?" I ask myself while my dentist works in silence. I run through a handful of scenarios in my head, fearing the worst, before Dr. J delivers the familiar and, in this moment, oddly calming refrain, "You need to floss more."

"That's it?" I ask skeptically.

"Well, it's clear that you don't floss as often as you need to, and I'm worried that might negatively impact this tooth." She points to an X-ray picture of my teeth.

At this point in the conversation I'm relieved about the news but, unfortunately, not any more motivated to floss after I leave. At my next appointment, though, I realize I should have acted on Dr. J's recommendation. It's too late; the cavity arrived, and my worst-case scenario has manifested.

SETTING THE STAGE

Much like this example of going to the dentist, feedback conversations put me in a headspace of overanalyzing and overthinking. The news I received from Dr. J about the state of my teeth was a form of feedback that I didn't respond to with the desired action—flossing more. As humans we often respond negatively to feedback, right? Even when doing so isn't in our best interests. Why is this the case? Why can helpful feedback still be ineffective?

In order to even begin talking about feedback, we need to discuss what we mean by feedback and how the concept has changed and evolved over time.

Before diving in, it's important to share that *Notice & Wonder* adopts three main types of feedback conversations that were first outlined in Douglas Stone and Sheila Heen's 2014 book *Thanks for the Feedback*. Stone and Heen preface the following kinds of feedback information with the idea that in conversations, "When we use the word 'feedback,' we may be referring to any of three different kinds of information:

1. Evaluation
2. Coaching
3. Appreciation

Each serves an important purpose, each satisfies different needs, and each comes with its own set of challenges." These various feedback conversations will surface throughout the rest of the chapter.

Starting by looking at *Merriam-Webster*'s online entry for feedback, the first definition that pops up is, "The transmission of evaluative or corrective information about an action, event, or process to the original or controlling source." This is the definition that is most closely associated with how we commonly think about and approach feedback. The primary purpose is evaluation. For example, this kind of feedback would include letter or numerical grades received in school or choosing "meets expectations" in a drop-down menu when you fill out your annual employee performance review. Essentially, this evaluation lets us know how we compare to the other students or coworkers.

However, interestingly enough, further down in *Merriam-Webster*'s feedback definition webpage there's a "kids definition" of feedback which I feel is actually closer than the primary definition of feedback for the purposes of this book, in terms of how it's framed in the pages that follow. As such, *Merriam-Webster*'s kid definition of feedback is, "Helpful information or criticism given to somebody to indicate what can be done to improve something."

While this definition doesn't include "evaluation" like the first, it's implied. Perhaps, at times, receiving a grade might be a motivator to study more. In a way, this definition expands the scope of feedback to emphasize coaching rather than evaluation. Coaching, as opposed to evaluation, often emphasizes suggestions and advice on how to improve performance or a process. Take my high school basketball coach, for example. While I didn't play in games very much, during practice he provided feedback on how to fix my crossover dribble or how I shot the basketball. In this way he exhibited coaching as a form of feedback, which ultimately helped me improve my basketball skills.

At a more foundational level, feedback is any information relating to performance or process. Yet, what we'll see in the next section is how the history of feedback—centered primarily in the workplace—is one that shifts between a strict focus on evaluation and ratings, and a focus on coaching and development.

FEEDBACK'S HISTORY

Feedback as a practice has existed throughout history. Although, it wasn't until the mid-1800s when "feedback" was used to describe the action of returning to an earlier point in a process. Feedback then emerged in physics when Karl Braun, a winner of the Nobel Prize in Physics for work on wireless telegraphy with Guglielmo Marconi, gave his acceptance speech, "Electrical Oscillations and Wireless Telegraphy," in 1909. According to *Merriam-Webster*'s Dictionary, feedback as a noun was adopted to describe the high-pitched frequency in audio output.

As feedback started to get adopted more and more into everyday use across different fields, there were related moments in history that shaped feedback as a practice, especially in the context of performance management. According to Peter Cappelli and Anna Tavis in their October 2016 *Harvard Business Review* article, during World War I and World War II the United States military created rating processes to identify and remove poor performing soldiers and a "forced ranking" system to identify and reward soldiers who showed potential to become officers. At this point the only interest was evaluation.

Around the same time, there was important research unfolding in Illinois that showed that how coworkers related to one another impacted their productivity in the workplace. According to Austin Weber's August 1, 2002, *Assembly* article, Elton Mayo, who conducted these performance research studies in the 1920s, observed the employees at Hawthorne Works, a large factory complex of the Western Electric Company in Cicero, Illinois. Mayo was brought to Hawthorne Works to study the impact of environmental characteristics, such as workplace lighting, on employee productivity and performance. Mayo and his collaborators found that social aspects of the work mattered more than physical environmental factors. Moreover, Weber noted that the findings from this research clearly indicated that, while evaluation and forced ranking seemed efficient in finding and rewarding the top performers, relationships in the workplace mattered, especially an employee's relationship with their supervisor.

Following World War II, the forced ranking approach gained extreme popularity and was adopted by many US companies, and as Cappelli and Tavis noted "about 60% of US companies were using them (by the 1960s, it was closer to 90%)." Cappelli and Tavis document in their *Harvard Business Review* article that in the late 1950s social psychologist Douglas McGregor suggested an alternative approach to this form of performance review, in which part of an employee's performance assessment would include a focus on improvement and development. Still, this approach did not catch on until much later.

Led by General Electric, there was a period of time where performance review processes added conversations focused on development. However, according to Cappelli and Tavis, this shifted in the 1980s under General Electric

CEO, Jack Welch, as he prioritized the forced ranking system and removed the employees that were considered underperformers and rewarded the employees who were seen as high performers. Prioritizing forced rankings persisted into the early 2000s, and at that point Cappelli and Tavis noted that "by some estimates, as many as one-third of US corporations—and 60% of the *Fortune 500*—had adopted a forced-ranking system." Following Welch stepping down as CEO in 2005, performance review environments across organizations made it a priority to take into consideration more consistent, developmental, and less formal feedback again. This trend appears to be continuing with organizations seeing increased promise in emphasizing coaching feedback over evaluation feedback.

While it was perhaps hidden below the surface throughout the ongoing shifts between evaluation and coaching, appreciation—the third type of feedback—did not seem to make an appearance that early. Appreciation, as stated in *Thanks for the Feedback*, "motivates us—it gives us a bounce in our step and the energy to redouble our efforts." Essentially, appreciation focuses on praise or affirmation.

Building on Stone and Heen's conception of appreciation, Therese Huston, author of the 2021 book, *Let's Talk: Make Effective Feedback Your Superpower*, added that at a deeper level, when voicing appreciative feedback, appreciation signals a sense of belonging. I know for me it's in these moments I feel seen by my coworkers and manager, which serves to build my trust in them. These are the moments of recognition, of calling out something I've been doing well and wanting to see more of in my deliverables moving forward. This combination of trust and moving forward, or making progress, are core features of effective feedback conversations, which we'll revisit throughout the book.

FEEDBACK'S EFFECTIVENESS

When pairing the alternative definition of feedback from *Merriam-Webster*'s dictionary mentioned earlier with the three kinds of feedback conversations, the question then becomes what kind of feedback are you looking for? What kind of feedback are you about to provide? Do you have a sense of whether the person you're entering into that feedback conversation with is anticipating receiving the kind of feedback you're intending to give?

In an ideal state, feedback provides an opportunity to motivate and/or improve performance, especially in the workplace. A 1996 *Psychological Bulletin* meta-analysis, conducted by Avraham Kluger and Angelo DeNisi, examined 131 research studies on feedback that consisted of a cumulative 12,635 participants. The findings found that feedback interventions had a positive effect on performance only 41 percent of the time, while still resulting in a negative effect on performance 38 percent of the time. In other words, feedback was just as likely to worsen performance as it was to improve it.

Moreover, Cheyna Brower and Nate Dvorak shared in their October 11, 2019, *Gallup* article that after receiving feedback from a manager that surfaced negative feelings, only one in ten employees reported continued engagement at work after that. Over 80 percent of the employees reported that they were less engaged at work after receiving criticism or feedback that left them feeling devalued, leading them to either passively or actively look for employment elsewhere.

Feedback ineffectiveness extends to the feedback giver too. In the same 2019 *Gallup* article by Brower and Dvorak only 14 percent of surveyed managers strongly agreed that they felt effective in their abilities to provide feedback. What's more is that Lou Solomon noted in a March 9, 2016, *Harvard*

Business Review article that according to a national survey that received over six hundred responses from managers, "A stunning majority (69%) of the managers said that they're often uncomfortable communicating with employees. Over a third (37%) of the managers said that they're uncomfortable having to give direct feedback about their employees' performance if they think the employee might respond negatively to the feedback."

What this demonstrates is that there needs to be more alignment between people engaged in feedback conversations. If managers are more likely to feel discomfort when communicating with their employees in general, and if employees don't feel motivated or engaged at work after feeling criticized by feedback they received, then we find ourselves in a feedback paradox. We know feedback is critically important—more on this in chapter three—but the intention and impact behind feedback remain disconnected at best.

I think the reason we struggle with conversations about feedback is because there's often a greater emphasis on the feedback content instead of the context in which the feedback conversation occurs. When this line of communication between manager and employee is weak, infrequent, or worse—nonexistent, it starts to make sense as to why feedback can be seen as ineffective.

FEEDBACK IN A TEAM SETTING

As I consider where this issue showed up in my own life, I think back to high school, when I was a benchwarmer for my school's junior varsity basketball team.

Practice after practice, game after game, I kept hearing the same refrain from my coach, "Marko, keep up the good work in practice, be prepared to see some playing time in tomorrow's game." Tomorrow's game always came, but my playing time did not. At a certain point it hit me that a lot of what my coach was saying felt like empty promises, and what made it worse was that I was becoming demotivated and starting to lose trust in him because of it. I was completely in the dark about my coach's decision-making process but grew unsurprised by the impact of it.

In this instance I wasn't looking for another squad to join because of feeling devalued by my coach, but I seriously considered quitting. When fielding the input from a manager or coach in the context of work, it's clear from Deloitte's 2021 Global Human Capital Trends report that employees put a premium on purpose and well-being; and I found in this top-down feedback loop with my basketball coach that his words weren't feeding into my sense of purpose or well-being.

After a few games where I saw no playing time the reality completely sunk in for me when I noticed that my jersey, even though I hadn't washed it in a while, still smelled like the dryer sheets that I used to wash it three games ago. It was in that moment I realized something had to change.

When I had this realization, I continued to try my best in practice but reframed how I watched the whole game from the sidelines. Instead of waving to my mom and shrugging my shoulders when she would ask from afar whether I was going in the game that night, I turned my focus to the game and began paying more attention to how our players on the basketball court were performing. This approach shifted my entire outlook on the game. I was overcome by positive internal-talk about how my teammates were doing, so much so that when they came out of the game we just started talking about what they were doing well and what I thought they should keep doing based on how it was working.

With this I was focusing on the group and not so much on if I was going to play. I started to enjoy riding the bench. As soon as I gained this perspective, and in a sense rejoined the team mentally, I was having fun, and I felt like I had found the community I was looking for.

In those moments when I was conversing with my teammates on the sidelines, I found a space in which I learned about the timing of when to share. When I got the timing right it usually coincided with a teammate initiating the conversation. More importantly, I saw two-way exchanges, true listening, and genuine interest emerge in these feedback moments.

FEEDBACK IS A TEAM SPORT

In the end, what I came away with after that basketball season was what I think would resonate with many organizations shifting their feedback processes toward coaching and more frequent and personalized feedback conversations. For feedback to be effective it needs to be built on "both/and thinking" rather than "either/or approaches." What I mean by that is as we continue to see this shift toward future-oriented coaching—as outlined in a 2019 *Gallup* article by Ben Wigert and Nate Dvorak—and frequent and personalized conversations—as suggested by Cappelli and Tavis in their 2016 *Harvard Business Review* piece—there needs to be balance.

Coaching with future progress in mind is crucial but so is engaging in evaluation of past performance. Similarly, consistent feedback engagement is an excellent practice to adopt, but only emphasizing individuals through this frequent and personalized approach limits how they contribute and impact their unit or organization as a whole.

Lastly and most importantly, building on the idea of moving away from either/or thinking, early on I primarily looked to my JV basketball coach for input, for decisions, and to provide that sense of cohesion. What I realized was that my experience with JV basketball went beyond this top-down relationship between me and my coach, and I became aware through my benchwarming conversations with my teammates of the power and decision-making abilities that we had. I began to understand how I could be most beneficial to my teammates and them to me, too.

I found community and empowerment on the bench. As the needle moves toward coaching and more frequent conversations, consider exploring how managers can empower individuals. Moreover, it's necessary to explicitly surface assumptions about who and how organizational decisions are made and examining who might be impacted by decisions about structures like feedback processes.

As you'll see in chapter two, an eye toward a sense of community and surfacing assumptions about decision-making and empowerment can prove to be the difference between feeling alone or excluded while navigating an already difficult workplace setting or harnessing the ability to stretch and expand your boundaries of navigating moments of feedback.

CHAPTER TWO:

THE IMPACT OF BULLYING

FEEDBACK'S MULTIPLE LEVELS

In the 1966 season one, episode two of *Star Trek: The Original Series*, "Charlie X", Captain James Kirk and Mr. Spock play a three-dimensional chess game—a futuristic take on the classic—where multiple chessboards are stacked in vertical levels. The idea behind three-dimensional chess is that it creates a more challenging game, which requires a high degree of attention to moves taking place across the different levels. Mr. Spock appears to be beating Kirk, but out of nowhere Kirk finds a way to checkmate Mr. Spock and win the game.

Much like three-dimensional chess, navigating a workplace is a series of ongoing interactions between levels, whether engaging with coworkers one-on-one, your team, or your department. Then, there's a level higher than that in which you may be interacting with the entire organization or a wing of your company. In short, interactions that occur at one level have various impacts at other organizational levels.

Feedback is a regular occurrence in the workplace, whether it's formal, like a performance review, or informal, which can consist of unplanned interactions with colleagues. What is said in these different versions of feedback can either motivate or discourage you. Not only the content of what is said is important but also *how, when,* and *where* it is given is as well. Context shapes feedback and, in a work setting, workplace culture and norms influence how a feedback interaction unfolds. In essence, there is a three-dimensional chess game taking place, with coworkers and context impacting a player's strategy.

Recall *Merriam-Webster's* original definition of feedback outlined in the last chapter, "The transmission of evaluative or corrective information about an action, event, or process to the original or controlling source." When we consider this definition we might think back to performance evaluation, where a manager might have told you that you've hit all your deliverables. But you may not be as much of a team player as you should be.

Perhaps it's the inverse, and you're getting along great with the team. There's a lot of chemistry but you're not pulling your weight at the individual level, and that's impacting productivity. In either case, both these forms focus on your efforts in the workplace and guide you to very specific solutions on how to improve. The important thing to remember here is the overall impact that the work environment has on the way you give and receive feedback, and even more so on your sense of purpose and well-being within your job.

This relates to my personal story traversing a different kind of feedback: workplace bullying. In my experience, I was dealing with consistent, subtle, but paralyzing actions that I had perceived were a direct result of me as a person.

Even though I was internalizing this "feedback" on the personal level, I found that it was also having a profound impact on my work performance as a result.

ORDER UP!

My first paying job was at sixteen years old, working at a restaurant that was attached to a shopping mall in southern New Hampshire. I was thrilled that I could make a little money, meet new people, and catch up with friends who stopped by before going into the mall; it was going to be great.

I walked into the restaurant wearing my white button-down shirt, black pants, nonslip grip Crocs shoes, and an American flag tie with the restaurant logo pinned to it. A woman in a dark grey pantsuit immediately greeted me. I found out a moment later that she was the general manager, Jane. After welcoming me on board, Jane told me that I was the youngest employee by three years. That didn't bother me, though. Instead, I was as excited as a child who had just received mail addressed to them for the first time.

I had a great time early on, but eventually I became self-conscious because I couldn't relate to anything my coworkers were talking about or their experiences. They always talked about what they were doing after work, who they were going on dates with, what bars they would meet up at, or whose party they were going to.

I noticed a shift in my confidence and the team dynamic when they began telling harsh jokes about me. At first I thought it was in good fun, so I just went along with it. But as the jokes continued, they became more severe and mean-spirited. I wanted to speak up for myself, but I felt like I didn't have any power in the situation. So, I swallowed my frustration, and I told myself, "Forget it; it's not worth it. I'll tell mom and dad when I get home, and they'll be able to help."

When I told my parents what was happening at work, they didn't believe me and perceived that sharing this was a way of complaining about having to work so much. What made it worse was that since they came to visit me on shifts and ate at the restaurant, they couldn't fathom that the servers and bartenders who are kind to them could be so mean to me.

My time at the restaurant only worsened when Jane was replaced by Tim, our new general manager. At face value Tim was cordial and friendly. However, he was often with a group of servers looking at me, pointing and laughing. I saw Tim's participation in the jokes as permission for the staff to continue making fun of me. This permission mixed with the false sense of inclusion he created and the fact that I was internalizing everything I felt, since it didn't feel like I had anyone to talk to about this, all hit me hard.

Then in the middle of a Friday night shift in January 2014, Laura, a cook, called me into the kitchen. Laura told me that she and the other cooks wanted to reward me for working so hard lately. She told me that they baked a personal brownie as a thank you and sign of appreciation for my efforts. At that moment I was overcome with immense happiness and finally felt like enduring all those challenging times at the restaurant was worth it, and I thought that my time there would improve.

Laura handed me the brownie. Tim and some of the other servers were in the kitchen gathered around me, waiting for me to take the first bite. I bit into what I thought would be a soft brownie but ended up being hard and crunchy. Everyone in the kitchen started to gag and burst out laughing. I was baffled, so I just started laughing too as I was trying to chew this brownie.

Suddenly, Laura told me that what I just ate wasn't a brownie at all. Instead, it was an old, burnt, and dusty french fry that one of the other cooks found while cleaning, wedged in the back corner underneath one of the stoves. They just concealed it in chocolate sauce. As she's telling me this, I slowly put down the plate, untied my apron, placed it on one of the kitchen counters, and left without saying a word.

The next day I went back to the restaurant to tell Tim I was quitting. In the four years I worked there I struggled with this internal narrative battle between continuing to try and find the positives in the experience, telling myself either that, "It will get better," or, "I'm learning something from this." At the same time, my coworkers consistently violated my trust, and I began to think to myself, "Maybe this is just how workplaces function." As a result I was becoming more and more discouraged and less confident in my abilities.

It didn't sink in until a few years after I quit, but I realized I had gotten the last laugh in what I was able to build at the local restaurant: resilience. However, I also came to recognize that that experience left some scars. One in particular that still creeps up every so often is the subtle and anxious paralysis in moments of feedback.

BULLYING: FEEDBACK BY ANOTHER NAME

According to a 2003 *Ivey Business Journal* paper, written by Gary Namie, "The term 'workplace bullying' was coined by the pioneering British journalist Andrea Adams in 1992." Gary Namie goes on to note that, "Dr. Ruth Namie and I introduced the term 'workplace bullying' to the U.S. in the popular press in 1998." As outlined in the introduction, and adopted from her 2003 *Human Relations* article, Denise Salin defined workplace bullying as "repeated and persistent negative acts toward one or more individuals, which involved a perceived power imbalance and created a hostile work environment." Behind these repeated and persistent negative acts are the enabling structures that run through the workplace. In short, just as the impact of interactions has a ripple effect across levels in an organization, so do the enabling structures and conditions that normalize behavior.

As I look back on my experience with workplace bullying in the restaurant, I realize I had convinced myself the ridicule was just part of the job, and it eventually became an enabling structure. A similar form surfaced when Tim gave my coworkers unspoken permission to make fun of me by joining in himself. In the April 20, 2021 episode, "How to Build an Inclusive Workplace", of the podcast *WorkLife with Adam Grant*, psychologist John Amaechi shared that, "I think [organizational] culture is defined by the worst behavior tolerated[...] And the act of doing nothing is what tells everybody it's okay." I realized that Tim's tolerance of the bullying and active participation was particularly challenging to overcome because Tim validated what the others were doing by watching from a position of power.

Mark Manson, author of *The Subtle Art of Not Giving a F*ck*, introduced what he calls the Feedback Loop from Hell. According to Manson, the Feedback Loop from Hell goes something like this: "You get anxious about confronting somebody in your life. That anxiety cripples you, and you start wondering why you're so anxious. Now you're becoming *anxious about being anxious.* Oh no! Doubly anxious! Now you're anxious about your anxiety, which is causing more anxiety."

For me, the Feedback Loop from Hell began with my perceived isolation at the restaurant. A 2012 research study published in the *Qualitative Health Research* by Kate van Heugten showed that among the impacts workplace bullying has on the targeted persons, it decreases well-being and increases anxiety and stress. I was stressed about the bullying, not speaking up, and feeling like I had no control. I worried about being stressed, and that was causing more stress. Considering that my early attempts to share these feelings were unsuccessful, this feedback spiral continued until I quit after four years.

The toxicity of workplace bullying is best summarized by Susmita Suggala, Sujo Thomas, and Sonal Kureshi in their chapter in *The Palgrave Handbook of Workplace Well-Being* published in 2021, "while observing at the organizational level, bullying impacts workplace culture, which alters aspects of the workplace in harmful and detrimental ways." In my case at the restaurant, it felt like a sense of community was being formed at my expense. In turn, a justification of unhealthy, unproductive, and exclusive norms and behaviors carried over into how other coworkers related to one another in the workplace more broadly.

At the core of my experience with workplace bullying was a lack of trust. As much as I tried to convince myself that things would be different the next time, things never improved. I didn't trust my coworkers or Tim. This is unfortunate for several reasons because research conducted by Paul J. Zak outlined in the January–February 2017 issue of the *Harvard Business Review* showed that "by fostering organizational trust, you can increase employees' proclivity and energy levels, improve collaboration, and cultivate a happier, more loyal workforce." My established lack of trust created discomfort and nervousness when I was around my coworkers, even in the moments where they didn't actively bully me, because I was always waiting for the other shoe to drop.

Only after I quit was I able to begin naming and making sense of my experience and feeling empowered by the resilience I had developed in the process. As I reflected on this, I couldn't help but hear the voice of Mister Rogers in my head and think about his TV show, where I and many other children learned about kindness, compassion, empathy, and listening. Mister Rogers, who also experienced being bullied, devoted his life to ensuring children had a positive outlet to name and make sense of their different feelings. This is important because his efforts to do so highlight an essential piece of the feedback process—setting the stage for everyone involved to feel a sense of belonging and well-being, regardless of what the feedback itself is.

RESILIENT MISTER ROGERS

Born in 1928, Mr. Fred Rogers grew up an only child in Latrobe, Pennsylvania, forty miles outside of Pittsburgh. As a child he was often sick and as a result was confined to his room much of the time. When he wasn't sick, he experienced childhood bullying.

Gavin Edwards, author of *Kindness and Wonder*, wrote that there was one day where Fred's school ended early, and his driver didn't know. Fred felt confident walking home by himself but along the way he realized that some classmates were following him. As Fred shared in Edwards's book, "It wasn't long before I sensed I was being followed by a whole group of boys." Fred picked up his pace but they stayed with him. "As I walked faster, I looked around. They called my name and came closer and closer, and got louder and louder."

Edwards continues Fred's account, writing that, "He ran, with a gang of bullies in hot pursuit, calling, 'Freddy, hey, fat Freddy! We're going to get you, Freddy.'"

Fred eventually evaded the group and made it home. As Fred continued to navigate adolescence and endure the ridicule, the advice he often received from adults close to him was a variation of, "Don't let it bother you," to "Don't show them it's affecting you, and they'll leave you alone," as noted by Edwards in *Kindness and Wonder*. This childhood experience would remain with him, eventually informing his desire to help children learn better ways to cope.

Toward the end of college, Fred was home on break and was in his house watching television, which at the time was novel technology. He was watching a goofy kind of show and thought that TV had extraordinary and profound potential to be a source of kindness, goodness, and learning. As a result, in the early 1950s Fred went on to become a producer on *The Children's Corner*, an educational TV show with puppets, songs, and music. While working on *The Children's Corner* he spent his free time learning from multiple child psychologists at the University of Pittsburgh, including Margaret McFarland—a Pittsburgh child psychologist who ultimately became a close mentor to Fred.

According to the April 30, 2018, *THIRTEEN* article written by Thomas Appleton, a year after *Mister Rogers' Neighborhood* aired nationally, and with the Vietnam War in full swing, the Nixon administration proposed reducing public television funds from $20 million to $10 million to support the war efforts in Vietnam. Fred, sitting in front of Rhode Island senator John Pastore, the chair of the Senate Commerce Subcommittee on Communications, provided a passionate and controlled argument for why public broadcasted television had tremendous potential to do good—as depicted in the 2018 documentary *Won't You Be My Neighbor*, directed by Morgan Neville. Moreover, Fred felt a responsibility to positively impact the growth and development of children through television and his program.

According to the documentary footage, on May 1, 1969, the last day of testimonies for the Extension of Authorizations Under the Public Broadcasting Act of 1967, Fred shared in front of the Senate Commerce Subcommittee on Communications that, "I give an expression of care every day to each child, to help them realize that they are unique. I end the program by saying, 'You've made this day a special day, by just your being you. There's no person in the whole world like you, and I like you, just the way you are.' And I feel that if we in public television can only make it clear that feelings are mentionable and manageable, we will have done a great service for mental health."

As Fred's testimony progressed, Senator Pastore became convinced of his argument and passion. Senator Pastore shocked everyone in attendance when at the close of Fred's testimony he said, "I'm supposed to be a pretty tough guy, and this is the first time I've had goosebumps for the last two days. Looks like you just earned the $20 million." After this *Mister Rogers' Neighborhood* took off.

Fred seemed to know that there was a direct connection between well-being and the formal and informal feedback interactions people navigate as they grow and learn. Fred always made it a point to demonstrate E.P.I.C. feedback characteristics, or Expansive thinking, Persistent conversation, Inclusion, and Compassionate listening in the space he created for his viewers. Due to this, there was the feeling that the viewer could learn about various topics through comprehensive and creative approaches, such as engaging with puppets and imagination. Fred met every question and comment raised by children with kindness and honesty, which allowed for ongoing conversation. A sense of belonging and community was the foundation of his vision and the message on which his program was built. Lastly, he demonstrated compassionate and generous listening on and off the air.

BUILDING THE PLANE WHILE FLYING IT

The feedback in the form of bullying that I received from my coworkers at the local restaurant stuck with me. As I experienced it, I saw its impact across different levels of the restaurant workplace, and I watched how behaviors normalized and became embedded in the workplace. Looking back on it now, it was as if I was building a plane while flying it. In other words, I was learning about the workplace while experiencing some of the most discouraging kinds of feedback someone can receive within it—a message of exclusion. I noticed this exact message was beginning to shape my understanding of what I thought other workplaces were like.

When I look at bullying as a form of feedback within that workplace, I consider the constant anxiety, the persistent stress, and the endless internal self-talk. However, as I think about these three things, I realize there wasn't a space to process any of it, a space to put a name to the things that I was feeling and explore the meaning behind those feelings. This is what made me think of Fred Rogers and his TV show *Mister Rogers' Neighborhood*. As a child Fred didn't have those spaces, either. However, he saw the potential to make sure others had that space to learn, process, and grow.

Much like Fred creating the change he wanted to see, or at least creating the change that he needed as a child, writing this book to help people process and engage in healthier forms of feedback is the change I needed to create because it's what was absent in my time at the restaurant. Fred's resilience showed in his understanding of how much he could challenge himself and continue to progress toward feeling like his viewers all had an E.P.I.C. space to engage in resilient-based feedback practices.

What I found out in hindsight after quitting my restaurant job was what Fred tried to ensure each child had, which was a space to process feedback at a younger age. Much like how feedback in the form of bullying stuck with me, Fred saw things such as kindness and empathy sticking with and impacting children as they grew up. In chapter three we'll dive deeper into this concept as I share when I realized that similar to Fred Rogers, I had the power to bounce back from my negative experiences, and that I could expand what I believed I was capable of in the face of feedback interactions.

CHAPTER THREE:

RESILIENT-BASED FEEDBACK

———

FEEDBACK FRACTALS

The last chapter discussed how feedback interactions play out on multiple levels. In my experience at the restaurant the individual interactions with coworkers decreased my sense of belonging and trust with coworkers, which carried over in similar ways at other levels. For example, when engaging groups of coworkers or when attending to guests in the dining room.

Another way to think about feedback interactions affecting you at different levels is to consider feedback a fractal-like space. A fractal is a concept in mathematics and science related to the connections between objects' small and large shapes within a system. Examples of familiar fractals consist of snowflakes, broccoli, and ferns. Author and activist Adrienne Maree Brown wrote in her book *Emergent Strategy*, "A fractal is an object or quantity that displays self-similarity, which means it looks roughly the same at any scale. Small-scale solutions impact the whole system."

Brown's definition of fractal resonates significantly in the context of being more aware of the shape of feedback engagement at a smaller scale within a personal or professional setting. The back and forth exchange created by feedback also speaks to its fractal-like form. These interactions have a spillover effect and reflect actions playing out at a larger scale of professional or personal feedback engagement. In short, you can learn a lot about feedback norms at a team or collective level by observing how feedback engagement plays out in one-on-one settings.

Suppose we become aware of the infrastructure that exists in different moments and levels of feedback. In that case, we'd be more adept at recognizing how that infrastructure facilitates and supports those interactions and dialogues. As a result, we'd be able to, at the very least, recognize familiar patterns when navigating different levels of an ecosystem. As Brown notes in *Emergent Strategy*, "What we practice at the small scale sets the patterns for the whole system." I think this is important because in the context of feedback it speaks to mindfulness, alignment, and sustainability. It's one thing to be intentional when approaching these three concepts, but that intention is only as good as the action and impact that accompany it.

In other words, acknowledging the fractal-like qualities of feedback spaces is important, but it will only get you so far. It's when that acknowledgment is paired with the recognition that patterns showing in moments of feedback speak to patterns emerging elsewhere in a personal or professional setting that you get further, and this is only the starting point! What we deem as a norm or feature in more minor-scale interactions shapes the contours of what's permissible or understood at a larger scale.

Approaching feedback as a fractal-like space allows you to make meaningful connections between noticing and wondering, in the middle of individual and team. In a similar light, I realized I could see how my negative interactions with individual coworkers were also playing out on a larger scale, which was evident in the toxic work environment that allowed for this bullying to take place. When I joined a team that promoted encouragement, motivation, and trust I could see and feel how this played out on a larger level by making me feel more productive and connected to the work overall.

What I've learned has profoundly shifted how I understand resilient-based feedback. A resilient-based approach to feedback doesn't happen in isolation: it's a phenomenon that occurs in a team context, rooted in community and collaboration.

FACING THE MUSIC

For a couple of years following my time at the restaurant the lingering effects of the workplace bullying I experienced there crept up in mysterious ways. They weren't always easily observable, but now and then they showed up as I navigated school, internships, jobs, etc. For example, I would over-apologize, or I would avoid eye contact when speaking—things that seemed annoying or rude at the moment, yet were actually just trained habits I had adopted to cope with being bullied.

The habit that hit home was the unpredictable pit that emerged in my stomach when engaging in feedback conversations. When I received feedback or any kind of criticism, I often had this intense anxiety, similar to being at the center of mean-spirited and severe jokes. Similarly, when giving feedback I was in the space of not wanting to come off in an anxious way. Sometimes it only lasted for a moment, and other times it lasted the entire conversation. The more I noticed the behaviors the more I realized that I was limiting myself in fully experiencing any given situation, of being present in the moment of learning, coaching, appreciating, and developing.

Then, I started a master's degree program in conflict resolution. I did my best to seek out experiences where I could practice observing and even confronting that feeling of anxiety, with the goal of harnessing that anxiety in order to reframe it in the form of appreciation or a deeper level of curiosity.

One day early in my first semester of the program I ran into my friend, Taylor. Out of the blue, she asked, "Are you interested in singing in a choir?"

A few weeks later I was walking into the first choir practice, despite my initial reservations.

As we were warming up, the choir director, Nolan, began organizing people into singing sections: bass, tenor, soprano, or alto. He put me with the tenors. I was overwhelmed, and those feelings of insecurity came back in a matter of seconds. "This time is going to be different," I told myself, and took a deep breath.

Once we finished a run-through of the first song, a tenor to my left turned to me and said, "Can we form a singing circle so that we can take cues from each other?"

"That's a great idea!" I replied as we invited the other tenors into this circle to sing more clearly and help one another work through the songs.

After our circle formed, I noticed it felt like we were really in this together, that we were there to hold ourselves and other singers accountable during practice in a supportive and communal way. I realized then that this was something that I had always looked for in the restaurant but never found: a sense of community. Seeing this sense of community starting to come together was the final piece that I needed to put myself at ease in order to embrace this learning experience fully.

I discovered very quickly that choir feedback flies at you a hundred miles per hour. You're constantly fielding formal feedback from the choir director and informal feedback, such as adjusting your singing pitch, key, or volume depending on how other sections are singing. As a result, my awareness and listening were turned up to the max.

We dove back into learning the first song with Nolan on piano. About a quarter of the way through the song Nolan purposely played a few incorrect piano notes and cut us off. "So, this is how each part is supposed to sound," Nolan said, as he began singing each part well. "This is how everyone sounds." He followed up lightheartedly and then began singing each part slightly off-key or a little flat. We all started to laugh at his imitation of our singing.

What was interesting about that moment was that he framed his coaching feedback so that we could see where we needed to be and then compare that to where we were. What's more, Nolan's imitation of our first try wasn't intended to be mean; it was meant to lighten the mood. This worked in the moment because he also said, "I didn't expect you to nail it on the first try. That's why we practice, and I know we'll get there."

The rest of the practices followed a similar flow, and we were starting to see noticeable improvement. By the time we got to the day of the concert we felt ready. Nolan commended us for putting in all this work, and he felt confident about our performance. After doing some warm-up exercises, we lined up and walked out on stage into the blinding, bright, indigo-shaded lights as people were taking their seats. I wasn't expecting the energy and excitement from the audience members, who were just as engaged in the songs as we were. Before I knew it the concert ended, and the audience was cheering and giving everyone a standing ovation.

In the short time that our choir was together (about ten weeks), Nolan created a community built on healthy feedback loops and trust. So much so that I have participated in this choir every year it has come together since my initial participation in 2015. From this experience, I realized that this choir created an ideal space for me to engage in a way that allowed me to turn off the internal doubt and take in all the feedback around me. More importantly, it showed me that I tend to learn more in moments of feedback than I notice or give myself credit for. Until joining this singing community I was paying attention to the wrong aspects of feedback, only focusing on what I couldn't control.

This is not to say that joining a choir is the silver bullet to becoming more resilient or expanding your ability to effectively engage with feedback. However, what I found with this choir experience was a space that allowed me to stop feeling bullied when receiving or providing feedback. There was a clearly defined and shared purpose in our singing, mutual respect and appreciation for one another, and a true sense that we were in this together. These were the ingredients that also helped me recognize my responsibility in sharing feedback with the other tenors when necessary. That kept me open-minded and in a present headspace when receiving input from the rest of the tenors, different sections, or the choir director.

SPREAD OF EFFECT

Merriam-Webster's Dictionary defines resilience as, "The ability to become strong, healthy, or successful again after something bad happens; the ability of something to return to its original shape after it has been pulled, stretched, pressed, bent, etc." In short, it's the ability to "bounce back." Resilience as a concept emerged most prominently in the 1970s, specifically in the context of ecology, but has since expanded across subject areas.

My experience with the choir adds to this definition in the context of feedback interactions by highlighting that resilience isn't experienced in isolation.

It doesn't only occur when something terrible happens or in moments of experiencing limiting or discouraging feedback, and it can expand your ability to navigate subsequent feedback interactions.

In the previous chapter I described my experience in the restaurant as essentially a lonely one. There was no trust between myself and my coworkers, and I navigated that space in a logical and tunnel-visioned way, meaning I just tried to focus on my job and then immediately go home when done.

Contrary to that experience, in the choir there was a strong bedrock of trust established, which created this feeling of "We're in this together and it's going to take all of us to be successful." This was empowering and, just like fractals, I noticed it had an effect on how I approached the music. I observed how this feeling spread across sections and brought us closer together as units, and then ultimately saw it engulf the choir as a whole. This spread of effect was ideal; I felt comfortable taking risks, like experimenting with harmonizing or risking a squeaky/cracking voice in an attempt to sing in higher octaves.

This spread of effect is also known as a positive emotional attractor (PEA). Richard Boyatzis, Melvin Smith, and Ellen Van Oosten, the coauthors of *Helping People Change*, frame PEA as a behavioral state that is triggered when positive emotions, such as fun, love, or excitement "activate the parasympathetic nervous system, which sets into motion a set of physiological responses that put a person in a more relaxed and open state." Being in a PEA state of mind opens the creativity and learning floodgates to support motivation and sustainable change. PEA can be thought of as amplifiers, so in a sense Nolan and the community of singers activated both our individual and collective PEA mind-sets during rehearsals.

According to a 2015 *Frontiers in Psychology* journal article written by Richard Boyatzis, Kylie Rochford, and Scott Taylor, PEA is balanced out by negative emotional attractors (NEA) defined by negative emotions—such as anxiety, stress, or fear—inducing a stress response and activating the sympathetic nervous system, limiting our capability to learn and shift behavior. In my time with the choir the NEA moments would consist of the final rehearsal and the concert itself, where we were all focused on carrying through what we learned to deliver a kick-ass performance. If PEA amplifies learning, then NEA can sustain it by locking it in.

The choir community was a ripe environment for resilient-based feedback interactions to surface. The last feature of this environment that made it so impactful was the ability to raise the baseline of where I saw my boundaries and constraints in the face of challenges. Dr. David Woods, a professor of Cognitive Systems Engineering and Human Systems Integration at Ohio State University, calls this phenomenon graceful extensibility. According to his April 2015 article in the *Journal of Reliability Engineering and System Safety*, Dr. Woods writes that graceful extensibility is "How a system extends performance, or brings extra adaptive capacity to bear, when surprise events challenge its boundaries." I see graceful extensibility as a feature that creates additional cushion when in feedback interactions.

The graceful extensibility that existed in the choir was the overall environment that supported failure in the face of taking risks, the feeling of trusting the other singers to cheer you on if you were successful in hitting that high note and laugh with you if you weren't. Much like my experience with the choir, these resilient-based feedback ingredients are cooked into one of my favorite TV shows *The Great British Baking Show*, which shows us how to bake expansive thinking, persistent conversation, inclusion, and compassionate listening into feedback.

BAKING IN THE FEEDBACK

The Great British Baking Show is a master class in resilient-based feedback interactions. Recall chapter one where we outlined the three types of feedback: Evaluation, Coaching, and Appreciation. If you've ever seen *The Great British Baking Show* you'll recognize all three types of feedback surfacing throughout the show in distinct ways. Each episode consists of three challenges: the personal bake, the technical bake, and the showstopper bake.

When the judges make their rounds during the three baking challenges, they share observations with the bakers about the different contestants' ingredient combinations they can't wait to try (appreciation). Or they ask the bakers questions to make them think critically about their baking process (coaching). Finally, at the end of the personal bake the contestants' bakes are ranked (evaluation), each receiving advice on what can be improved when baking that dish again (coaching).

While the judges' feedback is constructive yet hard, it is easy to observe the toll it takes on the baker. For example, following a challenging feedback interaction, a baker's confidence in the next round might be impacted. Perhaps they miss a step in the recipe, over- or under-bake something, or they might add salt when they should've added sugar (gross!).

What you can see play out next is why I consider the feedback interactions in *The Great British Baking Show* to be resilient-based: Even when a competitor is struggling or overwhelmed during a challenge, contestants swoop in to extend their assistance, support, and appreciation in this baker's moment of need—the TV show's version of graceful extensibility. Their support ranges from simply checking in and reassuring the stressed-out baker that they only received that harsh feedback last time because the judges know how capable of a baker they are, to helping the stressed-out baker achieve "small wins" within the time allotted for the challenge. And on the other side of those high-stress baking challenges, self-confidence, the sense of community, and support are strengthened. As a whole, this demonstrates to the bakers that they can experience a higher threshold of growing pains and push themselves a little further in the next challenge.

As mentioned in the last chapter, resilient-based feedback is a team sport. It's a combination of providing a particular kind of feedback at the right moment AND having a community of care behind you to support you along the way.

WHY FRACTALS?

Why is it worth exploring feedback, specifically resilient-based feedback, through the lens of fractals? As my experience with the choir showed, the impact and change started at the individual level. First, I gained trust and confidence in myself. Then, at that point I was ready to engage my group in a way that would replicate those feelings one level higher. None of this happened in isolation either; it was clear that the other bass, soprano, and alto sections were going through and experiencing that same process, culminating in us being able to carry the confidence, vulnerability, and trust in one another to the even higher level of the entire choir, cutting across the group and all singing parts.

The same holds true for *The Great British Bake Show*. It is, by definition, a competition. However, what's apparent very early on is that none of the bakers want to win at the expense of complete failure by the other bakers. As a result, a strong sense of community, trust, and motivation create the foundation of this competitive environment. Paired with the appropriate type of feedback, delivered to the contestants at optimal times in the competition, it's no wonder that by the end of the season it feels as much like a collective journey as it does an individual competition.

A resilient-based approach to feedback stretches boundaries of possibility, strengthens the ability to adapt, and expands the creativity pie. In the next part of the book we'll explore the characteristics of resilient-based feedback spaces more in-depth. For resilient-based feedback to unfold it's crucial to design E.P.I.C. spaces where feedback is rooted in Expansive thinking, Persistent conversation, Inclusion, and Compassionate listening.

PART TWO

PART TWO

CHAPTER FOUR

EXPANSIVE THINKING

——

THE ROAD MOST TRAVELED

We seem to take the same road routes that we always have, never trying a different path even if it shaves off time. When I go to Massachusetts to visit loved ones, without fail, I run into this problem—choosing the road most traveled. Often these routes aren't the quickest ways to get to destinations, but they are familiar to me. Years later I'm still discovering and ignoring faster ways to get to friends or family. Why is that? Why do I continue to take the route with the five to ten extra minutes' worth of trees?

This reminded me of a September 2008 research article written by Merim Bilalic, Peter McLeod, and Fernand Gobet, published in the international journal *Cognition*, that I had recently read. Their research demonstrated through chess how we have a tendency to choose familiar paths versus the more efficient ones, and I thought this to be a perfect example.

SOMETIMES EXPERIENCE OBSCURES POSSIBILITY

The researchers split chess experts into two groups. The first group received a chessboard with two paths to winning, a familiar route and a quicker route. The second group played on a board with only the efficient path to victory. The research demonstrated that group one could not locate the optimal checkmate path due to being preoccupied with focusing on the way they knew. Group two, however, was able to identify the optimal path due to not being distracted by recognizable checkmate paths.

This study represents the impact that the Einstellung effect can have when it comes to problem-solving. The Einstellung effect is the predisposition to solve an issue based on recognizable or familiar patterns that you've used to solve the issue in the past. However, that predisposition paralyzes your ability to see all options presented in your field of vision. This reduces your ability to think creatively or openly about an issue, or in our case, about feedback.

The Einstellung effect shows how bias can impact wide-ranging thought in feedback interactions and spaces. I believe that expansive thinking is a crucial step in ensuring feedback demonstrates meaningful impact. This kind of thinking emerges from being in a positive emotional attractor (PEA) state of mind—creating an amplifying and generative effect. At the core of expansive thinking in feedback interactions is the idea of fighting against biases such as the Einstellung effect and continuously working toward "Yes, and" thought, which can be understood as collaborative encouragement and recognizing small wins and their spread of effect in the process.

IMPROV & FEEDBACK

In comedian, actor, and producer Tina Fey's autobiography *Bossypants* she talks about her time at an improvisation company, Second City, early on in her career. She recounts learning valuable lessons and shares that while Second City was a "Yes, and" additive improv space, it wasn't devoid of prejudice, bias, and power asymmetries—which for Fey showed up in the form of gender discrimination.

Describing her experience working at Second City, Tina Fey noted the brilliance of her fellow comedians. She raised that her touring team would often substitute sketches provided to them with sketches and scenes they had written and were interested in testing with audiences. However, Tina Fey's caveat about Second City was that she experienced what she referred to in *Bossypants* as "institutionalized gendered nonsense," prejudice against women in the workplace. Fey gave the example of a Second City director once justifying cutting a scene by saying, "The audience doesn't want to see a scene between two women."

Fey shared another instance of this form of discrimination occurring later at Second City. She noted in the book that when she was there in the early to mid-1990s improv, casts included six members: four men and two women. As she recounts, "When it was suggested that they switch one of the companies to three men and three women, the producers and directors had the same panicked reaction, 'You can't do that. There won't be enough parts to go around, there won't be enough for the girls…' The insulting implication of course was that the women wouldn't have any ideas. I'm happy to say that the producers did jump into the 20th century and switch to a cast of three and three, and I got to be that third woman in the first gender equal cast."

Hearing Tina Fey mention her experience made me think more about the fact that it seemed even in "Yes, and" improv environments like Second City, enabling structures—as discussed in chapter two—can seep into any setting. In this case, gendered norms obstructed the possibility of proactively engaging feedback and impeded creative potential. Unfortunately, this isn't a new problem. A 2019 study conducted by Elena Doldor, Madeleine Wyatt, and Jo Silvester published in *The Leadership Quarterly* showed that, on average, women receive less actionable feedback useful for leadership advancement than men, which speaks to an inherent power asymmetry that shows up in the workplace.

Moreover, Fey's Second City story highlights moments of implicit "Yes, but" feedback—an enabling structure, and an instance of the Einstellung effect. In her book *The Improvisation Edge* Karen Hough wrote, "Monitor your 'Yes, but' activity. When you become aware of it, the words will begin to stand out in high relief. Understand that every time that nasty word 'but' shows up, somebody is being denied." Most notably, it seemed that the producers and directors who initially shut Fey's suggestion down were resorting to what, in their minds, was the "familiar path," regardless of how limiting and damaging that biased feedback was, especially in the context of Fey continuing to grow and improve at Second City.

As I think about how "Yes, but" feedback showed up in Tina Fey's experience, I started to think about where "Yes, but" was evident in my own life. It made me think about moments where coworkers ask for feedback to improve a project, but they are only looking for validation and appreciation that the idea's a good one in the first place, if not just looking for me to confirm what they already know.

These are the instances where after I've provided my input or sat through a brainstorming session, I think to myself, "Why ask me to workshop your idea if you just wanted it validated?" In these moments expansive thinking is just about confirmation bias rather than idea generation. As defined by *Encyclopedia Britannica's* online edition, "confirmation bias" is the tendency to select information and data that fit your argument or reasoning and exclude any information or data that doesn't fit. Still, in moments where the ask for input is genuine and a degree of progress is recognized and made, these are the moments that provide the satisfaction of small wins, which make a big difference in the long haul.

At the core of why "Yes, but" is detrimental to expansive thinking is the fact that, depending on the vantage point, it could look like it's bringing about progress or spurring motivation. Yet, as we explored fractals and feedback in earlier chapters, what may look like a step forward on one level might be two steps back at another.

THE IMPACT OF MAKING PROGRESS
The National Basketball Association (NBA), after pausing professional basketball games in March 2020 due to the COVID-19 pandemic, planned to resume games in a secure, isolated section of Disney World in Orlando, Florida, referred to as "the bubble." The coinciding protests over the countless murders of Black people by the police prompted the NBA and the National Basketball Players Association (NBPA) to come to an agreement regarding personal updates to their jerseys. Marc Spears reported on ESPN that all players were allowed to wear social justice messages on the back of their jerseys to raise awareness around the structural racism and systemic injustices faced by the Black community. This agreement between the NBA and NBPA was a continuation of NBA players joining in the protests and advocating for change, justice, and an end to police brutality.

Following the announcement of this agreement, Jimmy Butler, a professional basketball player with the Miami Heat, shared that he would like his jersey to only include his number, no last name or message on the back. Butler also expressed a degree of hope that the NBA would honor his choice.

An *ESPN* article written by Nick Friedell published on July 14, 2020, noted Butler sharing with reporters that, "I have decided not to [wear a message]. With that being said, I hope that my last name doesn't go on there as well. Just because I love and respect all the messages that the league did choose. But for me, I felt like with no message, with no name, it's going back to, like, who I was. If I wasn't who I was today, I'm no different than anybody else of color and I want that to be my message in the sense that just because I'm an NBA player, everybody has the same right, no matter what."

When games resumed on August 1st, 2020, Butler walked onto the court in a jersey with no name and no message, continuing to push for the NBA to honor his choice. Referees stated that the game wouldn't start until Butler changed his jersey, which he eventually did. After the game, reporter Marc Stein tweeted out the NBA's response which provided the rationale for why they had Butler change his jersey. According to the NBA statement, "Displaying no name or message on the back of a player's jersey was not an option among the social justice messages agreed upon by the Players Association and the NBA as modifications to the rules regarding uniforms."

What was the opportunity cost of not permitting Jimmy Butler to wear the jersey he wanted? The result of this decision did not negatively impact his ability to be a leader and advocate on and off the basketball court. However, the NBA's approach to Butler's decision raises a connection to the "Yes, and" versus "Yes, but" feedback interactions. This story sheds light on a missed opportunity to affirm Butler's broader leadership and create a space that allowed him to speak his truth.

Consider what Karen Hough noted in *The Improvisation Edge*, "A willingness to go with the idea of a trusted companion, support it, add our own creativity, and watch it play out may be one of the finest skills we can learn." The NBA took a proactive "Yes, and" step in working with the NBPA to generate options and ideas for players to advocate for different social justice messages on their jerseys. Yet, because of a "Yes, but" moment they missed an opportunity to learn from a trusted player and leader in Jimmy Butler and limited his individual growth within his workplace.

The small win of working with the NBPA created a chance for players to signal advocacy, solidarity, and support while playing in nationally broadcasted games. The importance of this is highlighted in a May 2011 *Harvard Business Review* research article where Teresa M. Amabile and Steven J. Kramer analyzed over twelve thousand workplace diary entries and found that, "Of all the things that can boost emotions, motivation, and perceptions during a workday, the single most important is making progress in meaningful work. And the more frequently people experience that sense of progress, the more likely they are to be creatively productive in the long run." Even though the NBA took a step in the direction of enabling "progress in meaningful work," they fell short when they met Jimmy Butler's idea/intention with disapproval, halting what otherwise could have built upon their small win and created an even bigger impact.

The above examples highlighted the shortcomings and missed opportunities of not fully embracing the concept of expansive thinking. When engaged fully, however, broad thinking enlarges the proverbial pie. Leaning into a "Yes, and" mind-set while recognizing and building on the progress of small wins can make all the difference in feedback exchanges. In brief, this mirrors an effective, win-win negotiation. When I consider this, I'm reminded of the fascinating instance in which the United States Postal Service (USPS) sued an indie rock band.

EXPANDING THE PIE

In the early 2000s, the USPS filed a lawsuit against an indie rock band for trademark infringement. The band's name? The Postal Service. The Postal Service was a band that had just come out with an album in 2003, amazingly enough, by using the USPS. The two band members mailed bits and pieces of songs back and forth through USPS from LA to Seattle until they completed the album. According to a November 2004 article published in the *New York Times*, "In honor of their working method they called themselves the Postal Service. Their album, 'Give Up,' was released by the Seattle-based Sub Pop Records in early 2003 and became an indie-rock hit, eventually selling almost 400,000 copies, the label's second-biggest seller ever, after Nirvana's 'Bleach.'"

The USPS filed a lawsuit against the band not too long after, which could've upended their album's success. As a result, they would have fallen victim to the Einstellung effect, just like the Second City directors and producers did in Tina Fey's story and the NBA did in their response to Jimmy Butler. Instead, the USPS dropped the lawsuit and permitted the Postal Service to retain their name in exchange for a notice on their album about the trademark and some much-needed publicity and marketing in collaboration with the band. By not following through with the lawsuit, the USPS found an opportunity to take a new and unexpected route which resulted in creative solutions to some of its marketing and branding needs and avoiding the detrimental impact that a lawsuit would have had on both the USPS and the Postal Service band.

Not recognizing continued moments of progress can impede creativity and expansive thinking, just as confirmation bias does. In addition to limiting open thinking, both concepts speak to the need to surface assumptions in feedback interactions to mitigate bias wherever possible. By explicitly noting assumptions, those in the feedback conversation create opportunities to reduce miscommunication about the type of feedback unfolding and increase a sense of shared understanding. When assumptions surface and become explicit they go from being a limitation to a creative constraint. In other words, they serve as insights to inform how best to go about acting on feedback.

CLOSING THOUGHTS

In resilient-based feedback interactions expansive thinking is about continuously working toward "Yes, and" spaces, making progress, and surfacing assumptions. Of course, this doesn't mean that every feedback conversation will be a positive one. Instead, this means that whenever navigating feedback it is best to approach it from the perspective of getting the interaction right instead of being right in the exchange, as this goes a long way in maintaining a capacity to generate ideas and options when the time comes.

Joe Hirsch raises the concept of "plussing" or additive thinking and writes in his book *The Feedback Fix*, "Just because we're selective about the feedback we choose to share doesn't mean we should limit where it leads. That's the essential point of plussing—to offer feedback that keeps ideas flowing, which, if done well, carries a huge upside: When there's no cap on possibilities, there's no limit on progress." This is a great idea in which to aspire. Still, as we introduced in this chapter, biases and assumptions can limit the ability to unlock this potential.

Expansive thinking is a core characteristic of actionable resilient-based feedback. It is generative, specific, clear, and purposeful. For resilient-based feedback to be effective and sustainable, however, it needs to be built upon in a persistent and ongoing dialogue.

In the next chapter we'll explore how persistent conversation is a defining layer of resilient-based feedback, one that creates an opportunity for accountability and legitimacy.

CHAPTER FIVE:

PERSISTENT CONVERSATION

———

RUN WITH IT

It's 5:00 a.m. on a Tuesday which in my opinion is the worst day of the week. My alarm is blaring, and my cat jumps out of bed as I stumble to turn the alarm off. Usually I do a guided run through a running app a few mornings a week, as part of my routine to gather and collect my thoughts and then to, oddly enough, let go of these thoughts.

I learned a lot about resilient-based feedback through running. First and foremost, I became aware that each run is unique and has an additive purpose, according to Nike running coach Chris Bennet in a July 2019 *Runner's World* article. For example, I may run the same loop in the morning but what I'm wearing might change, or it might be raining one day and sunny the next. Also, I could be running faster or slower, depending on what's on my mind. The point is, each run builds on the last and provides a new perspective or vantage point that I hadn't previously considered, either related or unrelated to running.

Next, there is no shortage of opportunities when looking for milestones and motivators on these runs, whether it's checking my pace and number of miles run or looking at a telephone pole or streetlamp up ahead and using it as a marker to run faster or slower once I've reached it. Motivation is what keeps me accountable to ensure I run for as long or as far as I said I would.

Lastly, I realized that there are moments where I need to slow down during a run so that I can speed up at a later point. For example, in the middle of a run I might need to decrease my speed from an eight out of ten to a four out of ten because always running at an eight would be difficult and unsustainable. When I slow down to a four, I instantly feel like I'm walking because it's nowhere near as fast as I was moving. As I keep running at a four, however, I begin to appreciate how well I ran at an eight. Moreover, slowing down provided an opportunity to pay attention to feedback from my body, like the shortness of my breath, the pain in my right knee, or discomfort in my left foot, and discontinue the run if necessary.

PERSISTENT & ONGOING CONVERSATION

Resilient-based feedback should be a two-way exchange of information in a cooperative manner instead of a competitive one. In other words, it should take the shape of a dialogue, and the two-way, collaborative nature of this conversation creates the conditions for relationship building and trust.

I think persistent and resilient-based feedback conversations in the form of dialogue create unique and purposeful interactions. No two talks will be the same, each provides greater perspective, and there is always intention behind each conversation, just like my 5:00 a.m. runs. For example, if my supervisor and I just had a discussion focused on coaching feedback, there should be measures of accountability in place to ensure I'm attempting to act on their input in good faith and they're voicing their appreciation of this effort. This could look like me sharing my progress or bringing related questions to my supervisor to demonstrate my determination to build on that feedback exchange. It also includes my supervisor following up with me to acknowledge and show appreciation that I'm attempting to receive the feedback. By the way, acknowledgment and appreciation go a long way in terms of motivation.

Expressed appreciation and acknowledgment of employee efforts by management is a powerful way to boost employee morale, retention, and productivity. This connection appears in a 2021 literature review conducted by Aisha J. Ali, Javier Fuenzalida, Margarita Gómez, and Martin J. Williams, published in the *Oxford Review of Economic Policy*. The researchers highlight the link between expressed gratitude and increased employee productivity. Additionally, this review called attention to the potential spillover effect of employees looking to demonstrate gratitude to others because of receiving it themselves. In other words, conveying gratitude motivates us and compels us to ensure others feel valued and that their contributions to their organization's efforts are meaningful too.

Finally, persistent conversation means being aware of the communication frequency or preferences of the other party/parties and moments where you or they need to step away from the conversation. Or even an awareness of times where you might all need to push through to achieve some shared understanding.

Much like from running and dialogue featuring purpose, accountability, and awareness, I've learned so much over the years from my friend, mentor, and former coworker Toddchelle Young about engaging in persistent feedback conversations.

MAINTAINING BALANCE

Toddchelle Young is the author of *Claim Your Worth Now!* and my former colleague at Georgetown University's Hub for Equity & Innovation in Higher Education, where she worked as the Director of Research for three years. We recently sat down to talk about the nature of feedback, and she detailed what she sees going into it, the layers and characteristics, and how she's seen feedback show up in her professional journey.

When Toddchelle started as an early career researcher in 2014, she worked with a supervisor she enjoyed. So, early on in that experience she wanted to make her supervisor proud and show her dedication to the work.

Toddchelle shared a story of how at 4:55 p.m. on a workday she was about to walk out of the office for the night with two big work binders of material to read later at home. Before she made it out the door, her supervisor stopped her and expressed, "I understand that you want to dive deeper into the work, and that's great. However, I do not want you to bring work home because you won't have enough time to do the things at home that you need to do, because you'll be so focused on working."

Toddchelle recounted that she was just amazed and speechless at hearing this—it was a revelation that what her supervisor mentioned was so intentional and is something Toddchelle still reflects on frequently.

Whenever they reconnect now, her supervisor still often asks, "What are you doing when you go home?" If Toddchelle replies that she has to bring work home, her supervisor will acknowledge that sometimes that might be the case. Still, she also reminds Toddchelle to find time for herself, by going to an art exhibit down at one of the Smithsonian's, for example.

It's that small act of holding on to that original piece of advice—not bringing work home—that I thought was an illuminating bookend. It showed what measures of motivation and accountability look like from the supervisor's perspective in how she navigates life after work, sharing some concrete ways Toddchelle could build that feedback into her after-work routine, and continuing to follow up with Toddchelle on this. This advice also made a difference in Toddchelle's navigation of the workplace. For example, even in our work together Toddchelle did not often work late because she finished what she needed to in a timely manner and held me to the same standard in meeting deadlines. As a result, the work surpassed the standards of quality initially set.

Following her experience where she stressed balance and well-being, Toddchelle found herself as a research consultant in South Africa starting in 2017.

LEARNING BY DOING

"So, I show up as a research consultant, which entailed me managing a team of seven research assistants. I didn't have much to go on. Either in terms of direction or how other colleagues managed the research assistants in the past."

Toddchelle knew she had to manage the staff, but she didn't have the tools or insight for being a manager in this role and context. This mattered for two reasons. First, the immediate need was for the research assistants to be engaged.

Second, Toddchelle knew that her supervisor would evaluate her at the end of this experience, and it mattered to her that she scored a good evaluation, and so she knew she had to jumpstart the work with her staff somehow.

She finally approached her team and started a conversation. Initially, she tried asking them about their research. Toddchelle recounted that she fielded nothing but silence and crickets. Then, she tried to learn more about what they were interested in outside of work, such as hobbies. Again, no replies.

She found that once the conversation finally began, none of the research assistants knew the definition or the focus of their work, tuberculosis and HIV, which Toddchelle found alarming. This gave Toddchelle the purpose and direction she needed to share with her staff that she'd be preparing presentations for the research assistants on the topics they would be engaging with until they received assignments from Toddchelle's boss at headquarters. She added that this coaching would include résumé workshops, which served as a deeper layer of motivation in ensuring her research assistants had what they needed to succeed after this experience, just as her supervisor had done early on in her career.

Toddchelle's coaching provided opportunities to deepen understanding and gave her a chance to engage the team until their assignment came through, which it eventually did.

This second experience highlighted two essential aspects of persistent conversations that can prove challenging: choosing to engage and ensuring accountability in the process continuously. For example, Toddchelle decided to initiate her work team's professional development without guidance, so her supervisors couldn't speak to how she could have built on successful components of her strategy. Similarly to generating my benchmarks and measures of accountability while running, there were no tools or resources to pinpoint how or in what way she could continue improving, so she created them.

This experience drives home that Toddchelle created a space where persistent and ongoing conversations built on what she learned from her first boss, and ensured purpose, accountability, and awareness with her employees in South Africa. Whether it's maintaining a healthy work-life balance or making sure your team has the skills they need to succeed, in the context of persistent conversations each exchange moves that effort forward in direct and indirect ways. Much like Toddchelle's experiences embodying characteristics needed for persistent and ongoing conversation, my former colleague Dr. Walter Rankin built on these lessons in a recent conversation.

PURPOSEFUL INTERACTION & EXCHANGE

Walter Rankin is currently the Vice Provost for Graduate, Professional, and Continuing Studies at Fairfield University. Walter worked at Georgetown University for almost ten years before starting at Fairfield. In his time at Georgetown, he first served as a Senior Associate Dean and then as a Deputy Dean and Senior Advisor to the Provost. At Fairfield, similar to his Georgetown role, Walter oversees the creation and launch of new academic programs, supports and provides guidance to students, faculty, and staff, and coordinates accreditation efforts and summer academic sessions.

As a colleague Walter always stopped to check in, even amidst overlapping meetings, competing deadlines, and being constantly on the move. He was always present and routinely paused, even if it was for a brief moment.

I learned from Walter that consistently slowing down is crucial, even for a brief moment, to acknowledge and check up on colleagues. That kindness has always stuck with me. I found that as I started intentionally taking routine pauses and checking in with my colleagues in those brief moments I also created a chance for me to re-center or recalibrate, to ensure that I was 100 percent present going into my next meeting.

Walter shared an instance when he worked with a faculty member to develop a brand-new program. As Walter recounted, this faculty member came to him with an idea for a new academic program focused on health. As a result, they began having follow-up meetings that unfolded throughout the year, brainstorming, talking through aspects of the program, and sustaining an ongoing conversation. This brings me back to how I began with the focus of Walter being intentional with checking in with his colleagues. This time it was directly related to his job responsibilities to ensure that this academic program was supported throughout the development process and successfully launched. So Walter describes these periodic meetings as a space where he and the faculty member had a sustained and ongoing conversation.

This space created an opportunity to build trust and motivation. Moreover, it provided a chance for Walter to suggest that faculty members either check out recommended resources or perhaps attend a conference to engage more deeply with program-related topics. He created this sense of accountability in ensuring that the faculty member could attend that relevant conference and continue building on what unfolded in these frequent conversations. I saw this example as an instance of Walter's process for developing and implementing academic programs.

Walter mentioned that there weren't any surprises in how this academic program finally played out. I think what was interesting about this aspect was that it seemed to stem from this constant and open line of conversation that unfolded periodically over the year because Walter and this faculty member were in continuous discussion. They were able to stay aligned and on the same page throughout the process. Walter did mention that if there are any surprises, "Then I've done something wrong." I took this as a nod to the accountability characteristic that I mentioned above.

PROCESS DEFINED BY INTENTION & IMPACT

Outside of Walter's kindness and its spread of effect, he has always stressed how necessary a process it is to ensure that all the affected people on campus have a stake in program decision-making and development. He shared that having a process in place that allows folks to have an opportunity to voice concerns or provide input is foundational. This reminded me of a piece that Walter coauthored with Jeremy Stanton, which was published on *The EvoLLLution*'s website in July 2016. The article, "Human-Centered Design in Higher Education", focused on what they had recently learned at Georgetown about how much of a difference it made in Walter's work for such academic program processes to incorporate a human-centered design approach.

According to a November 2015 IDEO.org video, human-centered design consists of creative approaches to problem-solving. It is a problem-centered and user-focused process, and it emphasizes iteration and designing solutions rooted in a deep understanding of the challenges or problems faced by the impacted individual, group, or community.

As noted in the IDEO.org video, human-centered design consists of three parts:

1. Brainstorming a range of creative possibilities for the impacted audience's needs and wants.
2. Building on this initial brainstorm of what's possible and feasible is learning more and deeply understanding the challenges or problems this specific audience faces. This part focuses on putting these ideas to the test, tweaking them accordingly, ensuring that the identified audience is the audience that continues to be emphasized throughout testing, and refining the creative ideas from the initial brainstorm.
3. Implementing those refined and tested ideas to show the feasibility of a way forward. A way that is again rooted in the needs and wants of the identified audience.

I mention this focus on ensuring program developments rooted in a human-centered design approach to drive home how Walter frames his process of working intentionally and collaboratively with his colleagues at Fairfield. As he notes in that 2016 article, "Within a higher education context, this audience-focused perspective helps align innovation initiatives with principles of student centricity, faculty support and development, and staff empowerment." In other words, Walter's process appears rooted in this inclusive focus, aware of the moving pieces and that those involved in the process are looking for support and belonging. I saw Walter continuing to stress this kind of program implementation process with his colleagues as an approach that works well for him. It clearly shows a connection between *intention* and *impact*.

CLOSING THOUGHTS

In the final minutes of my morning runs I often think about the "next starting line" rather than the current finish line that I'm about to cross. Whether that next starting line is the beginning of my workday or even the following day, I'm only finished running when I choose to no longer set out on my *next* run. Similarly, a persistent feedback dialogue only ends when you or the other party decides they no longer want to engage.

In both Toddchelle and Walter's stories they surfaced the core features of effective persistent conversations—purpose, accountability, and awareness—and spoke to a multiplier or spillover effect, which allowed them to apply these features to other conversation spaces and with a different set of stakeholders. Moreover, their insights speak to the uniqueness of each conversation in which they engaged. Every interaction either built on the previous discussion or provided a new perspective on the given topic.

Consider what was mentioned at the beginning of this chapter: ensuring persistent and ongoing conversation that's effective takes a lot of effort from all parties involved. It won't magically be a given after one feedback conversation. Instead, resilient-based feedback gets its power from intention and purpose, ensuring measures of motivation and accountability are in place to connect that intention to meaningful progress and impact. As we'll see in the next chapter, connecting purpose to impact extends far beyond any individual feedback conversation that leads to continued interaction, and focuses on building a sense of belonging and inclusion in which persistent conversation unfolds instead.

CHAPTER SIX:

INCLUSIVE BY DESIGN

SIDEWALK DROP-OFFS & RAMPS

In 1953 fourteen-year-old Ed Roberts contracted polio, which left him paralyzed from the neck down. Less than a decade later, in 1962, Ed—a wheelchair user since his illness—enrolled at the University of California, Berkeley. According to reporter Cynthia Gorney in an April 2021 99% *Invisible* podcast episode, the university was initially against him registering stating, "He was just too disabled. And where could he safely live? The iron lung, a respirator that provided breathing support—which he still used every night—wouldn't fit in a dorm room."

After converting a hospital room into a dorm room and thus being able to accommodate Ed, the university admitted him. At the time neither the university nor the city of Berkeley was accessible for wheelchair users. Ed relied on an attendant to push his wheelchair until he switched to a motorized wheelchair, which liberated him from needing someone to move around. However, he then faced the challenge of overcoming curb drop-offs from the sidewalk.

In the 99% *Invisible* podcast episode with Cynthia Gorney, Lawrence Carter-Long, the Communications Director for the Disability Rights and Education Defense Fund, shared that, "If you're trying to get across the street and there are no curb cuts, six inches might as well be Mount Everest. Six inches make all the difference in the world if you can't get over that curb." This barrier would turn out to be a spark that contributed to a significant civil and disability rights movement in which Ed would prove to be a leading voice and advocate.

Curb cuts, the slope in the curb that we see everywhere now, weren't a sidewalk feature much before the 1970s. That was until Ed and other students with disabilities formed an activist group called the "Rolling Quads." The Rolling Quads didn't want to wait around for reform to happen at a snail's pace, so among their forms of protest they would take sledgehammers and bags of concrete at night and turn curb drop-offs into ramped inclines for wheelchair accessibility.

This culminated in 1971 when the Rolling Quads went to Berkeley City Council to demand that they install curb cuts on street corners across the city. The vote passed unanimously, and the request was approved, creating the country's first curb cut program.

CURB CUTS & INCLUSION
Whether someone is pushing a stroller or lugging heavy bags, the curb cut unintentionally impacts them in a positive way, even though it wasn't designed with them in mind. This phenomenon of positive benefits from a user-specific design extending to others is actually called the "curb cut effect." It often surfaces in the context of inclusive design—designing a process or product with and for a specific

user. For example, as Emma Sheridan noted in a February 2021 "UX Collective" blog post, "Closed Captioning was originally created so that the deaf and hard-of-hearing could watch television. But today, people watching football games in loud bars or watching the news while at the gym benefit from captioning; and, we have the deaf community to thank for that."

Not only does resilient-based feedback put inclusive design at its core, it also creates spaces where the curb cut effect surfaces through building empathy and a sense of belonging. I believe that effective resilient-based feedback spaces and practices are uniquely curated for the individual or group that is being praised, coached, or evaluated. They do away with the idea of feedback as a standardized process and instead recognize it as a personalized, nonlinear, and dynamic experience that is person and context specific.

For example, while working at the restaurant I realized that the organizational culture didn't promote an inclusive environment. The feedback spaces were created by the very people who benefited from them. During my time at the restaurant the feedback in those situations left me discouraged and nervous about engaging in subsequent conversations.

Contrary to my restaurant experience, my time singing in the choir was characterized by inclusion and curb cut effects. There was a clear vision for us as a community that we were working and striving toward together. The feedback that we received always tied back to that vision in a way that promoted progress, a sense of belonging, and increased confidence in our ability to receive input from our choir director and the other singers. Moreover, the curb cut effects that surfaced in the context of increased trust in an otherwise vulnerable space created a level of authenticity that only strengthened over time.

Inclusive design is an essential characteristic of resilient-based feedback that amplifies the power of its two previous elements: Expansive thinking and Persistent conversation. In both cases, the way that plays out in a coaching session between my boss and I should look very different than how it plays out between my coworker and our boss. Even if my coworker and I have almost identical job responsibilities or have similar areas in which we want to grow, our identities are unique and our ways of working differ. Our comfort level engaging with our boss may also vary. The expansiveness of thinking and the persistence of conversation should therefore unfold in different ways. In this context, what inclusion does is twofold:

1. It's designed with and for the specific people entering the feedback space.
2. It builds a shared understanding, which is necessary to ensure feedback intentions connect to impact and action.

The benefits of designing feedback spaces for and with inclusion in mind extend to those outside that specific context. Much like how Kat Holmes, author of *Mismatch: How Inclusion Shapes Design* and Senior Vice President of Product Experience at Salesforce, frames inclusive product design in the context of designing with and for the needs of excluded communities. For resilient-based feedback to be effective, exclusionary practices related to giving and receiving feedback need to be identified and solved in each unique feedback interaction. In doing so, an opportunity to recognize how the value of a practical approach in one exchange could generate value in other spaces is created.

DESIGNING WITH & FOR END-USERS

Before joining Salesforce in 2020, Holmes played a central role in user experience (UX) and design at Microsoft and Google. Her expertise and passion center on accessibility and inclusive design in an increasingly technological age. Holmes grew up in Oakland, California, where she recounted awareness of diversity-related conversations from a very young age, mainly due to Oakland's diversity as a city. While she saw this as an opportunity, in a talk she gave at the Adobe 99U Conference, she noted that a focus on disability and accessibility were missing from the conversation.

Early on Holmes explored the arts and the sciences and saw the compliments that emerged when combining the two, which sparked her interest around what this all meant for accessibility and inclusion in design. She attended the University of California at Berkeley, where she majored in Biomechanical Engineering. Along the way, Holmes explored more deeply designing for inclusion and what that meant for people's relationship with technology. As a result of this curiosity, Holmes went on to oversee Microsoft's inclusive design and user experience (UX) efforts. Before focusing on scaling best practices related to accessibility at Google, Holmes published her book, *Mismatch*, which explores the intersections of inclusion/exclusion, inclusive design, intention, and impact.

One definition of inclusive design that Holmes offers comes from Susan Goltsman, coeditor of The Inclusive City, featured in a June 2016 Microsoft film. Goltsman offered the following definition: "Inclusive design doesn't mean you're designing one thing for all people. You're designing a diversity of ways to participate so that everyone has a sense of belonging." An inclusive design assumes there is no average user experience. So, approaching a design with a universal design focus, emphasizing the average user and a one-size-fits-all solution, can therefore create mismatches for anyone who falls outside of what's considered average. Similarly, resilient-based feedback starts with the idea that there is more than one way to design for effective feedback conversations.

When considering the difference between universally and inclusively designed feedback spaces, I think about when I was a student. Then, I always received low participation grades (or evaluative feedback) because the only form of participation outlined was speaking up in class discussions; projects and assignments didn't count as participation. So right from the start, I was always going to experience a mismatch because I didn't fit the average student that my teacher had in mind when the participation criteria were established. After all, I excelled with writing reports and working in small groups but didn't often speak up in class discussion.

This all changed in my very first class in graduate school. I walked into the class already assuming that I was starting at a "B+" at best due to participation being a feature in my grades up to this point. However, the first thing our professor said was, "There are a number of ways to demonstrate participation in my class and I acknowledge that for some that means regularly engaging in class discussion and for others it may mean referencing our class conversations in your papers and projects. I know everyone in this room has great ideas to contribute and I look forward to seeing them in whatever form they take."

Without even knowing this professor, I immediately noticed my nerves dissipate. While I still wasn't the most vocal in conversations, I became comfortable speaking up because I felt more in control of my participation rather than merely feeling obligated to contribute because of grade criteria.

MISMATCHED FEEDBACK DESIGN

Throughout her professional journey, Holmes noticed that everyone had unique ideas and understandings of what inclusion means whenever discussing it. As Holmes outlined in *Mismatch*, she came across the Latin root of inclusion and exclusion, "claudere," which means "to close or shut." Holmes goes on to note that, "It represents a literal enclosure, but it also represents a mental model of separation. The most common image that comes to mind is a boundary created by a closed circle." In short, she outlines the implications of inclusion, meaning "shut in," and exclusion, meaning "shut out," in what she called the shut-in/shut out model as depicted by an enclosed circle.

On the inside of the circle you have those who are shut-in, and on the outside, you have those who are shut out. She asks when considering this model, what's the purpose of designing inclusively? Is it to ensure those who are shut out can be let into the circle to benefit from resources and privileges? Is it to create a dotted circle or flexible boundary in which those who are shut-in and out can freely navigate between the spaces? Or is it to do away with the circle completely?

A core design principle for Holmes is designs that decrease mismatch. Designing for a one-size-fits-one rather than a one-size-fits-all immediately solves a mismatched interaction and creates a curb cut effect from which others benefit. In resilient-based feedback's E.P.I.C. framework, the "I" focuses on ensuring that the context of the feedback conversation is designed for a one-size-fits-one, individual approach. An example that Holmes uses to contextualize this is the invention of OXO kitchen tools, showing that the motivation behind the design was to overcome an observed challenge between people and the world around them.

Valerie Liston wrote about the story behind the OXO design in a January 2017 blog post on OXO's website. When Sam Farber noticed his wife, Betsey, having trouble with and experiencing significant discomfort from a vegetable peeler due to her arthritis, the idea of creating a more comfortable kitchen peeler design emerged. The Farbers worked together to design and launch a line of kitchen utensils in 1990 that featured an oversized, more comfortable rubber handle that was easier to grip. In this case, people who didn't directly experience Betsey's mismatch that led to the OXO utensil design ultimately benefited from its creation.

ONE-SIZE-FITS-ONE

With all this in mind, when returning to the shut-in/shut out model, Holmes shifts her original framing of the model to see it more like a cycle rather than an enclosed circle. We are continuously questioning design motivations, influences, features, and implications. This process begins with focusing on those most excluded. As Holmes stated in *Mismatch*, "Shifting that sense of exclusion requires careful attention to who's missing from a solution and from feedback channels. Whose voices are the loudest and whose are missing? Seek out who's missing and learn about their existing patterns of behavior."

Workplaces appear to be set up with a focus on the average employee's feedback experience. As we continue to design for "average," those who fall outside or deviate from that norm run into mismatches and are consequently left without a sense of belonging. As we consider the shut-in/shut out cycle, it's worth continuously exploring why, how, and in what way people are being shut out or excluded by current structures and norms related to feedback.

This highlights the value of establishing and situating feedback in a context of shared understanding. Developing a context of shared purpose and understanding in which feedback conversations can unfold aligns with what Dr. Ellen Van Oosten, an associate professor of organizational behavior and faculty director at Case Western Reserve University, described in our recent conversation as necessary conditions to establish meaningful relationships that facilitate connecting intention to impact.

It's worth noting that universally designed feedback processes and structures shouldn't necessarily be avoided. There are moments when feedback processes benefit from a uniform system. For example, consider performance evaluations. The structure itself is uniform, and the questions I'm asked are the same ones my coworkers are asked. However, the feedback should be situated in the shared understanding of my work motivations, strengths, and the areas of growth that my boss and I frequently discussed in the lead-up to my evaluation.

ESTABLISHING A SHARED UNDERSTANDING

Creating a shared understanding involves gaining clarity around the needs and preferences in that specific feedback space. This is a process that requires openness, trust, and a degree of vulnerability. As Brené Brown puts it in her book *Dare to Lead*, "Vulnerability without boundaries isn't vulnerability." That speaks to establishing an authentic context in which feedback can be transferred from one to another without running the risk of over-sharing or veering off course.

As a feedback giver, creating a sense of belonging and decentering yourself from the feedback you're giving achieves this. This way, you can ensure that you're entering the feedback space to better understand the needs and preferences of the feedback receiver without any preconceptions. Then in the following conversations you can dive into feedback exchanges because, at that point, everyone involved has a better idea of how to provide evaluative, coaching, or appreciative feedback specific to the other person.

Recall chapter three where Positive and Negative Emotional Attractors (PEA & NEA) were introduced. Dr. Van Oosten and her coauthors of *Helping People Change*, Richard Boyatzis and Melvin Smith, frame PEA as a reaction of the body and mind sparked by a positive feeling that positions us towards creativity and openness to learning. Dr. Van Oosten noted the following during our conversation on how PEA's impact surfaces: "When we truly discover and connect with our motivations and needs, we're able to be most authentic. When we're able to be most authentic and experience a kind of deeper understanding of ourselves and discover things that we care deeply about, this unleashes positive emotions that bolster us." In connecting this to resilient-based feedback, our graceful extensibility—the ability to support and stretch our feedback boundaries—expands when feedback aligns with and explicitly links to reference points, such as motivations. This creates the opportunity to identify clear connections between the feedback intention and purposeful and specific impact. Moreover, this reduces the likelihood of mismatched feedback interactions.

In their book, Dr. Van Oosten and her coauthors focus on becoming an effective coach and establishing meaningful coaching relationships rooted in compassion. They differentiate between the ideas of "coaching for compliance," which is often seen as short-term and goal-oriented, and "coaching for compassion," which is seen as longer-term and vision-focused. During our conversation Dr. Van Oosten described coaching for compassion as, "Other-focused and primarily about helping the other person discover and connect with their own ideas, their own feelings, their own hopes, their own dreams and then supporting them to reach the desired change. So you're trying to ignite an inner flame within the person," rather than meeting a short-term goal and "lighting a fire underneath them."

Feedback rooted in this context further speaks to the necessary conditions that spark an "inner flame," and the shared understanding that should emerge before any feedback interactions occur. It signals a mutual commitment by those in the feedback space to support and hold one another accountable in the process of engaging with and acting on feedback.

CLOSING THOUGHTS

Feedback spaces that aren't created through an inclusive lens and don't take a one-fits-one approach can't be characterized as resilient-based feedback spaces. Designing inclusively is hard work; it takes a good amount of reflection and perhaps even surfaces growing pains in the process. However, think back to fractals. How things play out in a feedback space has ripple effects, both positive and negative, across relationships, organizations, or networks. For example, suppose inclusion isn't the center of a feedback interaction. In that case, when you leave a harsh feedback conversation with your coworker or boss, you might feel discouraged or hesitant to engage in dialogue in other areas of work with different individuals. On the other hand, when that same difficult feedback conversation sits in a shared understanding of purpose or vision, and you both have an idea of your needs, you know you can leave that conversation having felt heard, valued, and like there are subsequent measures of accountability in place to ensure a connection to impact, large or small.

Developing the habit of noting effective feedback practices that may extend elsewhere is necessary for reducing mismatched interactions. As we'll see in the next chapter, a complimentary feature of this is compassionate listening. Compassionate listening, a characteristic of resilient-based feedback, fights against exclusion and mismatch by empowering those in feedback spaces to explicitly surface connections and important themes throughout their conversations to reinforce and build on their shared understanding continuously.

CHAPTER SEVEN:

COMPASSIONATE LISTENING

BACKSEAT DRIVING

No one likes backseat drivers. They're kind of annoying, and they distract you from paying attention to the road and the other drivers around you. I mean, seriously, when was the last time you enjoyed being told by a passenger to speed through a yellow light, or to make an ill-advised U-turn in a high traffic area because the passenger knew a "quicker route" to your destination?

Sadly, I'm ashamed to admit that I sometimes find myself "backseat driving" when others are behind the wheel. Through no fault of their own, when others are driving, I can't help but observe the misalignments in what I consider to be "good driving" and what others are demonstrating. It's probably a hot take, but there are times when I think my driving skills are better than others'. Whether that's the case or not is of less importance than the fact that my confidence is outweighing my actual driving abilities much of the time. While unfair, the reality is that when I backseat drive, I'm holding the driver to my driving standards, which may differ from their own.

Interestingly enough, I'm not alone. A 2013 research study by Michael M. Roy and Michael J. Liersch, published in the *Journal of Applied Social Psychology,* found that participants rated themselves as above-average drivers while at the same time believing that they would receive lower ratings from others. The participants' high ratings of their driving abilities were only based on their own conceptions of good driving. The study highlighted that participants were indeed aware that others might define good driving differently or include different criteria of what constituted good driving. Even when given a standard definition, however, participants still preferred their subjective criteria.

Much like how we rate ourselves in an inflated way against self-defined criteria when it comes to driving, we do the same when adopting a listening role in feedback exchanges. Again, this highlights the importance of creating a shared understanding in feedback spaces and following the agreed-upon standards and definitions of those involved when striving for a meaningful feedback interaction.

COMPASSIONATE LISTENING

When I think about it, I don't know that I was ever taught in school how to properly listen. I mean, sure, I got the occasional, "You shouldn't speak when someone else is talking," or, "When listening, always make eye-contact." However, there was never an opportunity to understand what listening with purpose entails and what defines effective listening. One of the more popular ways to differentiate listening types is by labeling them as passive or active. When we passively listen we basically enter into the conversation and don't make much effort to deeply engage or even show the other person that we hear them or understand what they're saying. We're probably thinking more about how we're going to reply rather than taking in and striving to understand what the other person is saying. Active listening, on the other hand, is just that: active. Active listening involves showing up to the conversation and being wholly present in the moment in every way—mentally, emotionally, and psychologically.

Compassionate listening, the last leg of the E.P.I.C framework, starts before the feedback exchange. This consists of preliminary discussions establishing agreed-upon definitions and standards of what meaningful listening looks like for subsequent feedback interactions. Following these early conversations, compassionate listening involves verbal and nonverbal cues and affirmations or clarifying questions to reinforce shared understanding and a degree of accountability in any follow-up interactions after the conversation to ensure continuous progress toward a defined vision, goal, or purpose.

Compassionate listening is the glue that holds the E.P.I.C. resilient-based feedback framework together because it involves:

1. Self-awareness to decenter yourself and move away from the default definitions and standards that you'd otherwise assess your listening and feedback against;

2. Asking clarifying and open-ended questions to gain understanding and surface themes, patterns, and connections that show the feedback conversation is aligned with the motivations and preferences of all parties involved and is moving toward a collective vision; and

3. Persistent conversation to learn how to best act on feedback received and/or how to continuously hold yourself accountable in supporting the person you just gave feedback to.

Recall Mara Mintzer and Growing Up Boulder's (GUB) work with children, introduced earlier in the book. What stood out to me about Mara and GUB's work was that it emphasized an ongoing process of engaging children in two feedback cycles with a range of city planning experts and officials, all rooted in compassionate listening.

EMPOWERMENT THROUGH LISTENING

Not only does Mara make it a two-way conversation with the children, but she also provides them the agency and autonomy to build on their own experiences, motivations, and preferences. The first feedback cycle focused on outlining the project for the children then pairing them with experts in the city planning space. This was a moment where the adults and experts decentered themselves to cocreate with the children to ensure alignment in defining the project's criteria and standards. Mara's example contextualized outlining shared expectations and an overview of a project and then connecting the children to experts.

Mara shared that, "We were working on designing some residential housing near a flood zone. The kids were trying to come up with ideas of 'How do you deal with the floods when water goes right to where that apartment complex was going to be?' After explaining the project, they engaged in a drawing activity to get their ideas down. They had these ideas like, giant salt fields that would absorb the water, and floating buildings."

As this first feedback cycle continued, the children engaged city planning experts. The experts assisted the children in reflecting on the feasibility of their initial ideas by asking open-ended questions that gave them opportunities to think aloud and gain a deeper understanding of their ideas.

At this point in Mara's explanation, it appeared that the first feedback cycle included a combination of surfacing assumptions and cocreating through open-ended questioning. This allowed Mara and her team to connect the open-ended questions to the children's answers and find common themes and patterns that helped clarify ideas in the second feedback cycle.

The second cycle involved the children sharing their work with city council members and other decision-makers. After the children captured their initial ideas and then engaged experts in the ideation phase, they synthesized and shared these ideas with decision-makers. During our conversation Mara noted, "We'll bring together city council members, the planning board or other commissioners, experts from the school district, and subject matter experts. The children present their final ideas and get feedback right then and there. Then, we create a report where we discuss the collaborative process of working with the children and highlight the themes we heard from them throughout the project."

What was so exciting about this was that through logging the children's ideas, patterns, and connections in a report submitted to the city council, there was already a layer of accountability built into the process on which Mara could follow up with children who were part of past efforts. "We gave that report to the decision makers and made it available to everyone, but it's most important, I think, for the decision makers, so that they can take it with them and actually implement it.

The last piece we did was follow up with the kids about what's happened with their ideas and how they've been either implemented or not." Sharing the final project outcomes with the children who contributed to them is challenging.

When children begin working on a multiyear GUB project they might be in second grade, but by the time the project is complete they may be in the sixth grade and no longer a part of the project or have moved away altogether. As a way to hold themselves accountable, Mara noted she and her team always upload project results to their website to keep the children informed and updated.

It was clear that compassionate listening and accountability measures are intentional features of these feedback cycles. Compassionate listening emerged when Mara and her team surfaced themes about their designs and work with the children. Accountability and transparency of process arose through Mara ensuring from a project's start to finish that the children who were a part of the project, even if they moved up a few grade levels, were notified of the final product and could see what they directly contributed to.

In her book *You're Not Listening,* author Kate Murphy wrote, "People who make an effort to listen—and respond in ways that support rather than shift the conversation—end up collecting stories the way other people might collect stamps, shells, or coins." Through demonstrating continued support rather than conversation shifts, Mara's team, the city planners, and city council members didn't just engage the children in an ongoing discussion, they also empowered the children in the decision-making process on the future of public spaces that they would be the ones using.

In a similar light, when we take part in feedback conversations, compassionate listening entails engaging AND empowering the person who you're sharing the feedback space with. Empowering the person receiving the feedback ensures that they have what they need to act on the feedback effectively. Moreover, this creates a space in which the receiver can clarify where and in what way they might need or not need support from the feedback giver. Finally, when done well the feedback exchange is authentic and genuine. As straightforward as this might sound, where we get tripped up is in trying to compassionately listen without acknowledging biases and checking bad listening habits at the door.

LISTENING TO SUPPORT, NOT SHIFT, THE CONVERSATION

The three aspects of compassionate listening—becoming more self-aware, gaining understanding, and providing intentional support—are necessary for meaningful interactions. As earlier chapters discussed, doing something effectively in one space impacts other personal or professional areas. Consider my experience with the choir when I finally felt like I regained my voice. That experience was impactful, and the feedback conversations I had in the process were purposeful. As I think back on it, I saw the three pieces of compassionate listening unfold in the choir but only made sense of them when noticing they were present or absent in other spaces.

Growing up, I learned that my voice sounds different to me than it does to others, which blew my mind. Fast forward to joining the choir. I thought I was a good singer based on how I heard myself and my generous self-assessments when singing in the comfort of my own home. However, I was brought back to reality during choir practices when hearing other sections and the collective singing made me more aware of when I was singing flat and off-key.

Nolan, the choir director, would often work with one singing group at a time, and the other sections would observe. For example, Nolan might start with the soprano section, working with them on what their part in a song sounds like, where to take breaths while singing, or how long to hold notes. While this happened, the alto, tenor, and bass sections paid attention to how their singing parts were similar, unique, and how each group complemented each other. Observing how our units complemented each other was where the choir's shared definition and standards of good singing emerged.

Through listening more to how the other choir sections sounded in specific songs and where my singing and their singing fit together, I started noticing when I was and wasn't doing that in different spaces. When in feedback conversations outside of choir, I thought more about things like, "How is the other person in this conversation hearing what I'm saying?" Or, "In what way(s) am I adding to a shared understanding in this conversation?" These questions helped me fight against the temptation to zoom in on an exchange and put myself or my perspective at the center of it. In the process, this created more chances for me to question my assumptions and not overestimate or overemphasize my understanding.

Due to this awareness giving me a chance to take a bird's-eye view of my choir experience, I became more curious when approaching our rehearsals. Also, I felt confident asking Nolan, as well as people in my section and other sections, clarifying questions like, "Why do tenors sing higher notes at 'x' point in the song, but sopranos sing lower notes?" Or ask about timing, like, "When am I supposed to harmonize or pause during the song?"

Oddly enough, I came to see this as a type of informal feedback that signaled to other singers if I was listening to them. If my timing or pitch was right then it sounded good, and if I was off, then it didn't sound good. I began to see more moments like this while navigating feedback interactions in the workplace. I thought more often, "Mark, you should W.A.I.T.," as outlined in Adrienne Maree Brown's book *Emergent Strategy*. Essentially asking myself, as Brown put it:

- "Why
- Am
- I
- Talking?"

Often when waiting, there will eventually be natural points at which I could ask for clarity and then mirror or reframe any aspects of the feedback in a way that moved the conversation forward. Asking with the intent to understand creates a feeling of reciprocity or a cooperative exchange of information. Due to the feedback conversation being two-way and something in which both sides invest, there's a deeper degree of sustained effort and support in feedback spaces.

Earlier in the book, when I shared my choir experience and its impact on me, I noted that when I arrived at the first practice Nolan mentioned we had a handful of songs that we had to learn in only four or five rehearsals. I figured this meant we needed to move quickly to make enough progress to feel like we had the songs down. Unexpectedly, we experienced the opposite—Nolan's feedback supported our ability to understand and learn while not feeling rushed by how much material we had to cover.

If one of us sang a song line incorrectly, or if someone asked for clarification on how a song section was supposed to sound, Nolan walked through the same song section for as long as it took for all of us to feel confident before moving on to the next section. He could have just as easily moved on to the next song and recommended other ways to get caught up. However, even in the face of limited collaborative time together, Nolan's feedback always supported rather than shifted the conversation.

Outside of choir, I used to find myself rushing straight to advice or solutions when a coworker or a loved one just wanted to vent, or trying to share a relatable moment when what they really needed was more open-ended questions. The point was that I wasn't doing what Nolan taught me to do: stay in the moment and support others the way they *want* to be supported as they work toward developing confidence instead of self-consciousness in feedback conversations.

In personal and professional feedback spaces, my impatience—before learning from Nolan—highlights that I assumed much and didn't notice that this was a big blind spot when trying to listen supportively to coworkers and loved ones. A 2010 research study published in the *Journal of Experimental Social Psychology,* by researchers from Williams College, The University of Chicago, and MIT, showed that while closeness can reinforce good listening practices because of trust and rapport built over time, we tend to overestimate our ability to listen with people we're close to. The research consisted of participants engaging in listening experiments with friends and then a second time with strangers. The research team found that participants overestimated shared understanding in conversation and their ability to communicate with friends rather than with strangers.

What this implies for compassionate listening is that even though listening to a loved one or coworker might seem easier to do, the closer we are to the other person the more quickly we assume that, because we had a shared understanding in one feedback conversation, a shared understanding will automatically be present in the next feedback conversation.

CLOSING THOUGHTS

Compassionate listening means listening to act. It begins before the first feedback conversation and even extends beyond it. This kind of listening emphasizes the intentional acts of decentering our own standards of what good listening includes, understanding how to ask context-building/clarifying questions in each unique feedback conversation, and supporting others while not overestimating what you think they need or want.

Compassionate listening continues as long as those in the feedback space engage intentionally to support the conversation. Likewise, support only arises through a sustained effort. This combination of sustaining and investing in feedback spaces is a core of compassionate listening and resilient-based feedback practices in general. What you'll find in the next part of the book is how specific audiences can sustain and support resilient-based feedback interactions.

PART THREE

PART THREE

CHAPTER EIGHT

STUDENTS & EARLY CAREER PROFESSIONALS

——

HYPEREXTENSION

In college I hyperextended my knee during a pickup basketball game. It happened so quickly. One moment, I was jumping to grab the ball after a missed shot and in the next, I was landing on the ground with a sudden and acute pain in my right knee. Oddly enough, after a quick moment of catching my breath, the pain went away, and I continued playing. However, I noticed I wasn't moving as quickly or jumping as high to get rebounds as I played on. While I could still play, I found it was hurting myself and my team.

Merriam-Webster's website defines hyperextend in the following way: "To extend (something, such as a body part) beyond the normal range of motion." Instead of resting and icing my knee, I kept going and stretched it in a way that went beyond its normal limits. The pain returned when I went to play later that week, but I just ignored it because I was motivated by the exercise rather than recovering. Every now and then I felt pain in my knee, even when I wasn't exercising. What's more, I became overly cautious because if I hyperextended my knee again, I might not be as lucky in being able to continue to play.

Since then, I find myself stretching and doing a lot more stability exercises before playing basketball to strengthen the muscles around my knee. By strengthening these muscles, I feel less pain there. In addition, I'm not overthinking or being overcautious when jumping and running. Overall, I know now that this self-care has benefits far beyond playing basketball.

HYPEREXTENDING YOURSELF

Much like this story, hyperextending yourself in feedback conversations is something to avoid. A feedback conversation could make you feel like you are bending over backward or going beyond your ranges of motion to give or receive feedback effectively. When receiving feedback, for instance, bending over backward might present as you feeling guilty if you don't continuously set aside your perspective or thoughts for the sake of the giver's opinions. Bending over backward could also manifest in becoming overly reliant and dependent on a particular individual's feedback. In addition, providing feedback in a hyperextended condition might look like becoming too involved, or sharing too much, which could detract from an effective feedback moment.

It's still doable to engage feedback in this hyperextended state, but it's less effective for those acting on it, and if left unchecked it creates unhealthy feedback habits. I should note that, to me, there is a difference between hyperextension and discomfort. Hyperextension in feedback spaces means paying no attention to boundaries, ignoring physiological signals from your body or mind, and still convincing yourself that you're present or engaged in the conversation. On the other hand, discomfort is feeling a sense of unfamiliarity during these conversations but allowing yourself to navigate these new terrains anyway. These moments can also provide you the opportunity to examine why your feedback boundaries are where they are in the first place and give you the chance to develop a stronger feedback skill set.

Just like adopting a regiment of stretching and strengthening the muscles around my knee, the same goes for exercising feedback muscles in ways that help sustain healthy feedback engagement habits and practices. As we explored in earlier chapters, the E.P.I.C. structure is what makes resilient-based feedback possible. Strengthening feedback muscles is challenging yet rewarding because beneficial practices and habits are created and sustained through ongoing and continuous effort. What I've realized is that the healthy feedback habits I've formed over the years are practices I look back on and say to myself, "I wish I started doing this when I was younger," or, "If I only knew this when I was a student or started working at 'x' job."

For this reason, the focus of this chapter is on resilient-based feedback practices for students and early career professionals. Specifically, focusing more on the E.P.I.C. feedback structure and how it provides those in feedback conversations with:

- Understanding that feedback engagement connects to well-being.
- Awareness that strengthening feedback muscles benefit from a trainer, or two, or six...
- Motivation to create and sustain healthy feedback habits.

This progression from wellness to autonomy creates opportunities to learn more about your feedback boundaries, so you are prepared to recognize and work against both hyperextending yourself or putting someone in a position where they might be hyperextended in feedback conversations.

SUSTAINING FEEDBACK ENGAGEMENT & WELL-BEING

When I'm in a pessimistic headspace due to experiencing a long time of only receiving evaluative feedback or only minor coaching and appreciation from my coworkers or loved ones, I find myself with little motivation to enter into any additional feedback conversations. Think back to chapter three where we explored positive emotional attractors (PEA), negative emotional attractors (NEA), and their implications. PEA and NEA exist in balance with one another; PEA amplifies curiosity, and NEA locks in what's learned from creative exploration. What's more is that the "balance" of PEA to NEA moments isn't one to one, and Barbara Lee Fredrickson, a psychology professor at the University of North Carolina at Chapel Hill, quantifies the degree of PEA vs. NEA moments that promotes greater well-being.

In her 2013 *American Psychologist* journal article, Fredrickson drew on past research of hers and others to show that "doses" of positive emotions should outweigh negative emotional doses in a day by a three-to-one ratio to support thriving and wholeness. In other words, although the negative feedback moments in our lives might be small, they're likely to stick with us longer and should be offset by more PEA moments that tap into our curious and creative sides and promote a sense of progress or motivation. However,

Fredrickson noted in her research that too much positive emotion could be damaging as well. "Whereas increasing levels of positive emotions bring benefits up to a point, extremely high levels of positive emotion carry costs that begin to outweigh these benefits." In short, too much of either PEA or NEA has detrimental effects. Because harsh feedback might weigh more heavily and perhaps limit performance, it's worth being mindful of and identifying frequent moments of recognition through appreciative feedback or strength building through coaching feedback rooted in encouragement and motivation.

As before, consider my experience at the restaurant where I was constantly fielding informal evaluative feedback, which put me in a fight-or-flight mentality at work. Since I didn't feel like I had much support at the time, I was more closed off outside of work. Reflecting on this experience I realized that well-being wasn't a catchall concept. There are multiple layers to it that are essential to explore. Relatedly, it's worth identifying which aspect of it means more to you at different points in time. *Wellbeing at Work*, by Jim Clifton—the chairman and CEO of Gallup—and Jim Harter—Chief Scientist for Gallup's Workplace division—outlined five types of well-being:

1. Career
2. Social
3. Financial
4. Physical
5. Community

Clifton and Harter argue that career is the most essential type because it's how and where you spend most of your day. As they note in *Wellbeing at Work*, "All things being equal, thriving in 'what you do every day' makes for stronger relationships, a more secure financial life, good health, and greater community involvement." While they see career fulfillment as core, they acknowledge that the other four kinds of well-being also impact your personal or professional endeavors.

At the local restaurant my career wellness was low due to dreading going into work, but what made things worse was my relatively low social well-being. I didn't feel support from coworkers and noticed my motivation was decreasing, and I was letting a lot of things affect me. As a result, my attention was divided when entering feedback spaces outside of work, and my responses and feedback weren't clear or specific. I began to pause and attempt to untangle my thoughts between what feedback I was about to engage with and what I may be bringing into that space.

So what did I do about it, and what can you do?

I began to ask myself a series of questions at various points throughout the process, and if I felt confident in my answers I would continue with the conversation. If I didn't feel comfortable with my answers, however, I would then discontinue the conversation.

Before engaging feedback, ask yourself the following:

1. Are there any motivators or stressors that might surface in this feedback conversation? If yes, what are they?
2. Will these identified motivators or stressors help or interfere with engaging a feedback conversation in an open-minded way?
3. How will I address my interests and the interests of others, so everyone feels included and heard in the feedback space?

During feedback conversations, explore this set of questions:

1. As outlined before from Adrienne Maree Brown's book, *Emergent Strategy: Shaping Change, Changing Worlds*, consider W.A.I.T.ing—Why am I talking? Am I building on or detracting from the feedback provided by either the other person or me in the space?

2. Am I compassionately listening, or am I just biting my tongue until it's my turn to speak?

3. Have we outlined how we'll follow up or continue this conversation?

After the conversation, think to yourself:

1. Am I holding myself accountable for what was discussed? Are those in the feedback space holding each other accountable?

2. If not, am I noticing any connection to one of the five well-being subcategories?

3. Am I wondering how I can support or be supported?

These aren't the only questions that you might pose to yourself, but they are the ones that speak to sustaining E.P.I.C feedback conversations, and they help to keep you in a resilient mind-set in the face of feedback. While these might be worth exploring at the moment, developing stronger feedback muscles takes time, patience, and an intentional team built by you to improve your ability to engage ongoing feedback.

SUSTAINING FEEDBACK TRAINERS

Improving and strengthening your feedback muscles also takes a village of trainers who all bring their perspectives, areas of knowledge, and ways of working into the feedback training regimen. For this book, the suite of trainers is called a people wheel, a term that I came across in a January 2020 LinkedIn blog post written by Amy Philbrook, Head of Customer Care, Learning & Development at Robinhood. A core lesson from Amy's post on creating your people wheel is that it's pretty difficult to accomplish goals independently, so surround yourself with people who broaden your perspective, challenge you, and support you along your journey toward achieving something. In our case, our journey is continuously building up our ability to navigate feedback in an E.P.I.C. way.

According to Philbrook's blog post, in a professional or personal context, a people wheel consists of six trainers:

1. **Mentor**—Someone who has more experience than you do and is someone you might turn to in the face of a tough decision.
2. **Coach**—Someone who can help you work toward a specific goal or vision.
3. **Subject Matter Expert**—Someone who broadens your perspective by bringing unique knowledge or understanding to the table.
4. **Sponsor**—Someone who "goes to bat" for you, who advocates for you.
5. **Truth-Teller**—Someone who isn't going to sugarcoat. You can always trust this person to cut through the fluff, get to the point, and provide honest insights.
6. **Reverse Mentor**—Unlike a mentor who helps in the decision-making process, a reverse mentor might make the decision-making process more difficult as they often bring perspectives to the table that hadn't been considered before.

HOW DO YOU GO ABOUT BUILDING YOUR PEOPLE WHEEL?

In short, it takes intention, cooperative exchange, and strategy when considering the various people wheel roles. First, identify those who you think would be an excellent fit for one of your trainers. Once identified, reach out and look to connect. This requires time and may take multiple conversations, but if you genuinely engage with them and invest in that emerging relationship, it will pay off. I've found that, generally, people want to help.

When you've established that relationship, consider the following questions:

- Which aspects of feedback can this trainer help me with as I look to develop skills or deepen knowledge in my undergraduate major or in the professional field I want to pursue after I graduate?
- How might I show that I'm holding myself accountable to their guidance and lessons?
- How can I ensure that I don't take offense at negative feedback or resort to cutting ties with someone in my wheel (namely sponsor, truth-teller, or reverse mentor) if they provide feedback that I don't agree with?
- How frequently should I turn to them?
- Who might I replace them with if one of us moves or switches jobs?

Your people wheel will change, but that's okay! We constantly change and adapt to new environments, like a new classroom with a new professor or a new organization with different coworkers and managers. It only makes sense that those who helped you earlier in your journey may be a different group than those best positioned to help you now.

The core function of this team is to ensure that you are engaging feedback in constructive and mutually beneficial ways.

SUSTAINING FEEDBACK PRACTICES

Building on well-being and constructing your people wheel is the idea of developing and sustaining resilient-based feedback habits. When you consider my experience with the choir, for example, at first being social was a significant stressor, like when working at the restaurant. Still, it quickly turned into motivation when I unintentionally surrounded myself with coaches, mentors, reverse mentors, sponsors, subject matter experts, and a truth-teller, all within the choir community. During practices the ritual we got into consisted of having Nolan play the song, rehearsing section by section; Nolan, as choir director, provided critical coaching or appreciative feedback. Then we all sang the song together. This takes the category of a ritual because the order and meaning of events follow one another, rather than a habit that might be something that routinely occurs for you, but the sequence of habits is flexible.

What comes from this emphasis on sustaining habits and rituals is that it helps us become aware of what we might already be doing well, and it highlights where we need to improve or change and adopt a new practice altogether. You can go about doing this by:

- Engaging your people wheel frequently and intentionally. You've built a network of people invested in your growth and development, so make those relationships and your time with them worthwhile.
- Being specific in where and how you'd like to improve in that aspect of feedback. Communicate to those on your

people wheel with whom you'd like help with this. It will alert them to look for signals for follow-up interactions with you so they can speak to potential improvements you might be making.

- Asking someone in your people wheel, who might be a student peer or coworker, if they could provide some feedback to you on your last deliverable or project. Similarly, gauge if they feel comfortable with you giving feedback to them on their previous assignment. In both cases of practicing to receive and give feedback, begin these conversations with those in your people wheel network.

- Expanding and branching out to engage people outside your people wheel, other coworkers, or loved ones. When branching outside of your core people wheel, repeat the steps. Communicate the specific area that you're working on, intentionally engage in feedback conversations, observe the new muscle being built around existing habits or forming around new habits or practices, and combine these practices with what you've learned throughout these interactions.

- Realizing your own ability to give and receive timely E.P.I.C. feedback. You'll develop a clearer sense of your boundaries and how to remain accountable to yourself and others in feedback conversations.

Interspersed throughout these steps are moments of pause so that you can make sense of what you're learning and understand how things you're learning fit together. Just like building your people wheel, creating beneficial feedback habits and practices takes time, patience, and strategy.

PRACTICE MAKES PROGRESS

The flow from wellness to learning from your people wheel only reinforces the development of sustainable feedback practices. Most importantly, pay extra attention to *how* you adopt a new exercise or training regimen because how you start sets the tone for your progress. In addition, this progression from well-being to autonomy creates opportunities to learn more about your feedback boundaries. This better prepares you to recognize and work against hyperextension in feedback conversations.

Sustaining resilient-based feedback practices takes time and effort. However, while it was mentioned in this chapter, it's worth stating again that upholding the techniques on your own is, by definition, unsustainable. There needs to be support from those inside and outside of your people wheel to provide guidance and create feedback environments where you can not only build up your resilience but also flourish and thrive.

In the next chapter we'll explore how those who you might consider trainers can ensure that they're assisting you in a way that demonstrates growth.

CHAPTER NINE:

EDUCATORS & MANAGERS

CAN I VENT?

Have you ever gone to a loved one or coworker to vent about a stressful situation or general frustrations, and instead of listening they try to offer solutions? They think they're supporting you through sharing unwanted advice of what they think you're looking for and ignore what you want or need, which is just for them to provide validation and listen. When I've experienced the phenomenon of being met with unsolicited advice, I've gotten more frustrated or increasingly stressed as a result. Moreover, the other individual often becomes defensive, and in rare occurrences gets mad at me for getting frustrated with them.

I'll admit, I've been on both sides of this, and I suspect you have too. In instances where I've been the one offering unwanted solutions, I'm not listening or considering what the other person needs in terms of support. It's as if I'm thinking to myself, "Why won't you just let me be a supportive friend?" I'm waiting for my friend to finish venting so I can share my advice, suggestions, or solutions. Simply put, I make it about me. As soon as I make it about myself whatever trust or motivation my friend had before the conversation instantly dissolves.

Ensuring effective and meaningful support means when it comes time to show up for others, I'm able to set aside, to the best of my ability, any thoughts or responses that make it about me. As we'll see in the rest of the chapter, strengthening and sustaining effective feedback habits depends partly on those in supporting roles who are fully present and create an empathetic and nonjudgmental space for others to learn about and establish their healthy feedback practices.

THE OTHER SIDE OF THE FEEDBACK COIN

In the last chapter we explored the nature of creating and bolstering healthy and beneficial feedback habits from the perspective of students and early career professionals. Maintaining helpful feedback norms is hard work but should not reach to the extent of hyperextension. While it holds for everyone navigating feedback, for those in structured learning contexts like students in a classroom or early career professionals in the workplace, encouraging feedback habits takes hope, kindness (to self and others), guidance, and most importantly, support from their people wheels and networks. Educators and managers play essential roles in supporting their students or employees in feedback spaces.

In many ways, this chapter and the previous one mirror each other to denote two sides of the same coin, sustaining and supporting. For educators and managers, the three areas to emphasize while working on the application of resilient-based feedback habits are situated in how to provide effective support when considering:

1. Feedback engagement and its connection to well-being.
2. Feedback context and mind-set shifts.
3. Feedback-rich environments and their impacts on understanding and growth.

At the core of this chapter is the hope that if educators and managers don't already see their methods and modes of working reflected in the supportive feedback habits below, then they have the opportunity to explore how and in what ways they might incorporate them into their unique contexts.

SUPPORTING FEEDBACK ENGAGEMENT & WELL-BEING

At a former retail job, I had a manager who was a passionate leader but often bore an excessive amount of responsibility. While at first I was enjoying the work and exceeding expectations, after a while I found myself tired and disengaged when leaving meetings with this manager, to the point of frequently looking for new employment following these experiences.

When I realized our meetings were no longer as beneficial as they could have been, or had been, it suddenly clicked for me why: my manager was experiencing work burnout. A May 2019 news release by the World Health Organization noted that burnout is, "A syndrome conceptualized as resulting from chronic workplace stress that has not been successfully managed." Due to this and the general sense of fatigue that developed, I felt like every time I met with my manager I was receiving less and less actionable feedback.

This instance highlights the spread of energy and emotions and its mutual impact on wellness in the context of career or purpose—enjoyment in what you're doing day in and day out. While this example only scratches the surface of the details behind this spread of effect, what's worth noting is that my supervisor's experience with burnout had profound impacts on my well-being as an employee. I'm sure distancing myself and being less communicative didn't boost their wellness either. Moreover, this connects to what Jim Clifton and Jim Harter wrote in *Wellbeing at Work*, that manager and direct report well-being are linked. A change in either the manager or employee's well-being can affect the other's ability to thrive.

Recall from the last chapter the emphasis on students or employees taking a moment to gauge their well-being levels before feedback encounters. The same internal assessment holds true for you as an educator or manager. Before engaging feedback, consider exploring the following areas:

1. Establishing and communicating your well-being and self-care boundaries. This all begins with answering the question, are there moments in your day or week in which you can reclaim time to focus on yourself? Effective feedback relies on honesty, trust, and a degree of vulnerability, each of which require exploration into where and how you define your feedback boundaries.

2. Reflecting on your own preferences and needs in addition to thinking about the other's preferences and needs in feedback spaces. This allows you to frequently and internally assess where your needs and motivations do and don't align with the shared understanding or purpose of a specific feedback moment.

3. Connecting and building on what you've learned from navigating previous feedback exchanges. Each feedback engagement produces a wealth of information. It's as much on those in educator and manager roles as it is on the others in feedback spaces to connect that new information with what went well and/or how they might improve their feedback effectiveness this time around.

I believe educators and managers are often overworked and under-resourced in their positions. This was especially visible during the COVID-19 pandemic, which forced us into remote and online learning and working from home. As such, to provide effective support before, during, and after feedback conversations, educators and managers must also support their own well-being.

SUPPORTING FEEDBACK AS A TRAINER

As Dr. Ellen Van Oosten shared when we were in conversation about managers as coaches, "Unless [managers] are clear what it means to coach, they approach it, or are influenced largely by how they perform the rest of their jobs. They might bring more of an evaluative perspective to coaching. So that's where I think the nuance here is that we see all of these as part of coming underneath an umbrella of helping relationships, but one has kind of distinctive qualities or characteristics." Both educators and managers play a variety of roles in their respective work environments. They take on roles such as advising, coaching, mentoring, evaluating, etc. What sticks out as a common thread across these functions is that while they might share overlapping traits, all of them require a unique set of skills and knowledge to do them effectively. Similar to shifting your mindset and articulating the kind of feedback conversation you're about to have with others in the space, the same needs to be done when switching between roles as an educator or manager.

A way to guide your trainee and the support you're providing is to explore the following questions throughout your time helping someone cultivate effective feedback habits.

1. What is the student's or early career professional's vision for developing more beneficial feedback practices? Who do they want to be in three, five, or ten years?

2. Is your support visible or invisible? Are you reading the situation correctly?
3. How will you know that your support was beneficial? How might you hold yourself and others in the space accountable?

I understand this line of questioning as an iterative process that happens in the pre-feedback conversation space. Recall the people wheel for a moment. At times managers or educators take on different training and supporting roles for peers, early career professionals, or students who have brought them into their feedback habit development. As such, I believe it's necessary to clearly vocalize the kind of support you're providing to someone working toward sustained beneficial feedback habit or change. This starts the process of reading the feedback space or interaction and ensuring that how you're approaching your support is aligned with the role you were selected for in someone's people wheel. As Dr. Van Oosten shared above, be mindful of how your other roles might be influencing your ability to coach or mentor effectively.

SUPPORTING FEEDBACK PRACTICES

Supporting those in strengthening their feedback muscles is an effort that takes place on three fronts. First, yourself. We discussed above the importance of recognizing where your emotion contagions surface and making it a point to support yourself before supporting others. Second, others in the feedback space. After ensuring that you're in an excellent space to provide support, ensure that you're aligning your support and training to the kind of feedback habits that someone is attempting to build and sustain. Third, the feedback environment. Consider this kind of support as being fractal in nature. As we've talked about before and as is a running theme throughout the book, what happens at a smaller scale or on an internal level impacts how things unfold at a larger level or in externally facing spaces.

Organization Science published an article written by Constantinos Coutifaris and Adam Grant in August 2021 exploring their research in creating psychological safety in the workplace and its connection to managers asking their teams for feedback. They found that managers who displayed vulnerability and openness about the evaluative feedback they've received on past performance created a feed-back-rich environment for their employees, more so than managers who didn't show the same level of vulnerability. This research highlighted an amplified version of emotion contagion, where the manager displays a degree of openness and leads by example. This culmination is a critical aspect that builds on the earlier sections and eventually establishes a feedback-rich and supportive environment.

Recognizing and providing frequent appreciative feedback as a manager or educator builds on the above ideas of openness and vulnerability. What I've realized is that it's easy to get lost in the personal or the professional. When paired with a minimal appreciation of what might be going well, that can take a toll on my mood, work quality, or even my overall presence in spaces. I think back to the professor I had in grad school who shared that he sees value in other forms of class participation.

Each week this professor called on one of us and shared in front of the class what he found interesting, inspiring, or promising from one of our writing assignments. We would do this before jumping into that class's conversation. It may seem relatively minimal, but I can say that for me such recognition is energizing to continue building on what I might be doing well, and it's contagious. In addition, fielding appreciative feedback from a manager or educator makes me more inclined to keep an eye out for moments where I might support others in feedback conversations more effectively and do the same in vocalizing or sharing appreciative feedback with others.

PROVIDING BENEFICIAL SUPPORT

Educators and managers play important roles as leaders, connectors, and supporters both formally and informally. When in spaces where students or early career professionals are attempting to uphold beneficial feedback habits, providing effective support rests on educators and managers:

- Taking care of their own well-being before supporting others in feedback practice and improvement.
- Learning more about what feedback habits need to be adapted, and shifting your role and way of working accordingly.
- Normalizing vulnerability and recognition in feedback environments.

When managers and educators are open to engaging authentically, a feedback moment is created that interrogates what it means to be authentic in your support and shared accountability, starting at the individual level and eventually permeating the workplace or classroom. However, developing and sustaining E.P.I.C. feedback structures, spaces, and processes won't happen overnight, and we won't get it right every time, but that's not the point. What matters is that when we acknowledge our own position, purpose, and accountability to ourselves and others when engaging feedback, we're that much closer to creating E.P.I.C. feedback spaces that foster a sense of resilient collaboration and community.

CONCLUSION

———

WE'VE ALL BEEN THERE

Feedback is an essential aspect of everyday life, whether it occurs in personal or professional spaces. Unfortunately, as we saw earlier in the book, actionable feedback that leads to improvement is often the exception rather than the norm. Between the unease or stress from anticipating feedback and its ineffectiveness, I sense many people leave these conversations feeling troubled like I did when I experienced workplace bullying in my first job. The problem with the current view of feedback is that it can be beneficial when it's done well and is vital for growth and improvement; however, it remains ineffective as a process. Moreover, as we saw in chapter one, the history of feedback has been connected with a sense of needing to change for change's sake rather than exploring sustainable and purposeful feedback systems.

What originally started as a process to improve my ability to tell stories quickly turned into sharing more of my own story than I had intended to convey. I was called to write this book because, through my experience of finding what resilient-based feedback means to me, I realized that feedback exchanges are more complex than they may look. Effective feedback conversations start a few steps before receiving appreciation, coaching, or evaluative feedback. Thus, I felt compelled to name this and share the connections I've made from my own experiences to feedback-related research and literature.

Most of us, if not all, have been in situations where we've felt bullied by feedback, whether it's feeling overwhelmed by needing to deliver critical input or the uncomfortable pit in your stomach when receiving discouraging insight. Notice & Wonder is about feedback rooted in resilience: Resilient-based feedback. The layers and characteristics that make up resilient-based feedback don't speak to the feedback content; these characteristics emphasize the context in which feedback is delivered and received. Resilient-based feedback is an E.P.I.C. process that focuses on the "basics" of creating feedback spaces that are:

- **Expansive**: approaching feedback conversations openly and creatively.
- **Persistent**: ongoing conversation that establishes a consistent and clear line of communication on which to build.
- **Inclusive**: creating a sense of community and belonging through feedback exchanges.
- **Compassionate Listening**: listening in a meaningful way that surfaces clarity and understanding.

FOUNDATIONAL FEEDBACK CHARACTERISTICS

There's a reason that we are all introduced to these four concepts (expansive thinking, persistent conversations, inclusion, and compassionate listening) at such a young age. It's because they're foundational for what makes up purposeful communication, which has the potential to bridge disconnects and build mutual understanding. Engaging feedback in an E.P.I.C. way creates a whole that is greater than the sum of its parts. In other words, E.P.I.C. feedback settings get their power from the four concepts working in partnership. When combined, the additive impact motivates, sustains, and supports beneficial feedback habits and practices.

Part one centered on why feedback is often ineffective, how my experience with workplace bullying connected to feedback, and why taking a resilient-based approach to feedback can deepen its impact. In addition, we saw that feedback's history and barriers continuously change. Lastly, we were introduced to a framework to overcome such obstacles.

Part two reviewed the resilient-based feedback framework and the characteristics of what goes into it. When combined these pieces complement one another and allow meaningful and actionable feedback to take shape.

Part three concerned the practical application of resilient-based practices. First, through strengthening and sustaining healthy feedback habits in students and early career professionals. Next, ensuring that educators and managers are mindful of their role in student or employee feedback growth and development.

What surprised me most about this endeavor was the noticing and wondering I continuously encountered along the way. While writing, primarily part two, I experienced the very takeaways I hoped to instill within my readers and I met the same feedback challenges, such as the Einstellung effect or "Yes, but" thinking, that I'm sure you'll eventually encounter and successfully overcome.

FEEDBACK TAKES A VILLAGE

Writing about feedback was an exciting experience mainly because it connected the dots as to why my physiological responses in specific feedback settings are defined by fight-or-flight reactions. In contrast, in other feedback moments my body's response promotes creativity. Writing Notice & Wonder and immersing myself in what I found to be the features of resilient-based feedback expanded my understanding of where my assumptions and biases are when in feedback spaces and how to work against those blind spots.

The amount that others have invested in my book, listening to me talk at length about the ideas behind my writing, sharing their time, personal stories, and insights has been awe-inspiring, energizing, and humbling. I continue to be floored by the fact that it takes a village to write a book and how many people stepped up to help.

This process had a significant impact on the way I write and tell stories. Before writing Notice & Wonder I didn't realize that I wrote in an inaccessible way that didn't allow for—as we discussed in chapter six—a diversity of ways of engaging with any topic that I was writing about. In short, I didn't write inclusively and what's worse was that I didn't know it. This feeling of now knowing some details of my own writing in general sparked curiosity and hope that this experience was going to be worthwhile, and it was.

ROOTS & BRANCHES

Notice & Wonder provides a unique perspective and angle on how to approach feedback spaces and conversations. I hope this book challenges you to notice the complex and often unexplored roots of engaging feedback and wonder how feedback branches from one conversation to the next.

Relatedly, I hope that you acknowledge the immense ripple effects that feedback exchanges can have in other aspects of personal and professional settings.

Applying resilient-based feedback practices is deceptively tricky. However, as these feedback muscles strengthen over time, I hope Notice & Wonder positions you to identify and perhaps demonstrate resilience in feedback spaces. More importantly, making connections that build on this resilience creates feedback settings that promote a sense of flourishing.

ACKNOWLEDGMENTS

——

Writing *Notice & Wonder* was a journey of determination, vulnerability, and gratitude. The stories, experiences, and connections that make up the book required a degree of openness that initially I wasn't ready for. Even so, as I shared in my chapters, emotions and feelings are contagious. So when I saw the excitement of my family, friends, and colleagues before I even wrote the first pages of the book, I felt motivated and confident that the result would far exceed any expectations that I set for myself at the start of this journey.

Throughout the editing process I found that I was going through the learning pains of improving my own display of expansive thinking, persistent conversation, inclusive design, and compassionate listening during the feedback interactions I was having with editors. At the same time, I was making a case for this E.P.I.C. feedback framework's immense value. As such, this book would not be what it is without the kindness, generosity, and substantive and actionable feedback provided by so many.

First and foremost I'd like to thank my partner, Emma Ridings, for your unwavering support and the countless conversations you withstood about half- and quarter-baked ideas that went on to be refined and helped shape the narrative and core arguments in *Notice & Wonder*.

Thank you to my family, especially my mom and my dad, Sara and Jack Joy, for being there for me every step of the way. To my older siblings, Cristina Mirshekari and John Joy, and my brother-in-law, John Mirshekari, thank you for always looking out for me, making me feel heard, and for your indispensable advice and guidance.

Thank you to the *Notice & Wonder* beta readers, Darryl Jones, Diana Jarek, Jenni Duever, Zach Omer, and Emma Ridings, for your time and dedication to improving the book's content through your honest insights and remarkable feedback.

Thank you to New Degree Press, Eric Koester, my fantastic editors, and all who played a role in creating and publishing *Notice & Wonder*. To Elissa Graeser and Mozelle Jordan, what a journey! Thank you both from the depths of my heart.

And thank you to everyone who participated in a personal interview, supported my preorder campaign, and helped me create a book I only ever dreamed of writing. You have all made publishing a reality, so thank you for this, and for noticing and wondering with me.

Anel Patricia Albertao, Hayley Aron, Samantha Bartelson, Lauren Blood, Taylor Bologna, Bob & Anne Borrelle, Bobby Borrelle, Matt Brooks, Mary Kate Buckley, Chris Chacko, Colleen Chiochetti, Chelsea Cooper, Hamid Darbandi-Fard, Myrthe Doedens, Claire Donald, Amy Dong, Jenni Duever, Alexa Eason, Lada Edwards, Heidi Elmendorf, Rebecca Eppler, Yasmine Fawaz, Dan Folger, Michael & Michelle Fontaine, Jeff & Renee Fontaine, Danielle Fontaine Caban, Nicole Fontaine Dooley, Theodore Freudenberg, Nichole Fusco, Brittany Gore, Kelly Gregg, Benjamin Hack, Lionel Harris,

Maria Hernandez, Diana Jarek, Linda Johnson, Darryl Jones, Margaret Joy, Jack & Sara Joy, Bill & Mary Pat Joy, John Joy, Stephanie Kapinos, Ellen Kapinos, Courtney Kelly, Amy King, Eric Koester, Abigail Lewis, Michael Lloyd, Destiny Lopez, Kevin Lu, Ben Manzione, Noah Martin, Susannah McGowan, Jan Menafee, Gabby Mikalonis, Rachel Milner Gillers, Mara Mintzer, John & Cristina Mirshekari, Ray Mirshekari, Mary Mirshekari, Molly Morrison, Ijeoma Njaka, Kaye (Mawge) Ogilvie, Zach Omer, Alex Ortiz, Rita Owens, Michelle Pea, Duncan Peacock, Gaby Perla, David Peters, Kate Phillips, Walter Rankin, Allie Rastelli, Tom Reilly, Mike Ricci, Emma Ridings, Barry & Luann Ridings, Curry Ridings, Lowell Ridings, Michael Ridings, Csaba Roszik, Jacob Segal, Greg Skotzko, Rajiv Sonti, Dana Tandilashvili, Jake Trickett, Adam Twardowski, Tad Umali, Ellen Van Oosten, Robby Weiss, Caroline White, Mia YH Cook, and Toddchelle Young.

APPENDIX

INTRODUCTION

Bradford, David, and Carole Robin. "Why Feedback Often Doesn't Work." *Thrive Global*, March 5, 2021. https://thriveglobal.com/stories/why-feedback-often-doesnt-work/.

Braund, Taylor A., Donna M. Palmer, Gabriel Tillman, Heidi Hanna, and Evian Gordon. "Increased Chronic Stress Predicts Greater Emotional Negativity Bias and Poorer Social Skills but Not Cognitive Functioning in Healthy Adults." *Anxiety, Stress, and Coping* 32, no. 4 (2019): 399–411. https://doi.org/10.1080/1061 5806.2019.1598555.

Gemzøe Mikkelsen, Eva, and Ståle Einarsen. "Relationships Between Exposure to Bullying at Work and Psychological and Psychosomatic Health Complaints: The Role of State Negative Affectivity and Generalized Self-Efficacy." *Scandinavian Journal of Psychology* 43, no. 5 (2002): 397–405. https://doi.org/10.1111/1467-9450.00307.

Hawi, Nazir S., and Maya Samaha. "The Relations Among Social Media Addiction, Self-Esteem, and Life Satisfaction in University

Students." *Social Science Computer Review* 35, no. 5 (2017): 576–86. https://doi.org/10.1177/0894439316660340.

Huston, Therese. "Giving Critical Feedback Is Even Harder Remotely." *Harvard Business Review,* January 26, 2021. https://hbr.org/2021/01/giving-critical-feedback-is-even-harder-remotely.

Kätsyri, Jari, Teemu Kinnunen, Kenta Kusumoto, Pirkko Oittinen, and Niklas Ravaja. "Negativity Bias in Media Multitasking: The Effects of Negative Social Media Messages on Attention to Television News Broadcasts." *PloS One* 11, no. 5 (2016): e0153712–e0153712. https://doi.org/10.1371/journal.pone.0153712.

Kluger, Avraham N., and Angelo DeNisi. "The Effects of Feedback Interventions on Performance: A Historical Review, a Meta-Analysis, and a Preliminary Feedback Intervention Theory." *Psychological Bulletin* 119, no. 2 (1996): 254–84. https://doi.org/10.1037/0033-2909.119.2.254.

Mintzer, Mara. "How Kids Can Help Design Cities." Filmed November 2017 at TEDxMileHigh, Denver, CO. Video, 14:15. https://www.ted.com/talks/mara_mintzer_how_kids_can_help_design_cities/footnotes?language=en.

Salin, Denise. "Ways of Explaining Workplace Bullying: A Review of Enabling, Motivating and Precipitating Structures and Processes in the Work Environment." *Human Relations (New York)* 56, no. 10 (2003): 1213–32. https://doi.org/10.1177/00187267035610003.

Seldin, Melissa, and Christina Yanez. "Student Reports of Bullying: Results from the 2017 School Crime Supplement to the National Crime Victimization Survey. Web Tables. NCES 2019-

054." *National Center for Education Statistics* (2019). https://eric. ed.gov/?id=ED596357.

The United Nations Children's Fund. "What Is a Child-Friendly City?" Accessed August 23, 2021. https://childfriendlycities.org/ what-is-a-child-friendly-city/.

CHAPTER ONE: FEEDBACK EFFECTIVENESS

Braun, Karl Ferdinand. "Electrical Oscillations and Wireless Telegraphy." Nobel Prize Lecture, December 11, 1909. Accessed August 23, 2021. https://www.nobelprize.org/uploads/2018/06/ braun-lecture.pdf.

Brower, Cheyna, and Nate Dvorak. "Why Employees Are Fed Up With Feedback." *Gallup, Inc.*, October 11, 2019. https://www.gallup. com/workplace/267251/why-employees-fed-feedback.aspx.

Cappelli, Peter, and Anna Tavis. "The Performance Management Revolution: The Focus Is Shifting from Accountability to Learning." *Harvard Business Review,* October 2016. https://hbr. org/2016/10/the-performance-management-revolution.

Deloitte. "The Social Enterprise in a World Disrupted: Leading the Shift from Survive to Thrive." *Global Human Trends.* Accessed August 23, 2021. https://www2.deloitte.com/content/dam/insights/ us/articles/6935_2021-HC-Trends/di_human-capital-trends.pdf.

Huston, Therese. *Let's Talk: Make Effective Feedback Your Superpower.* New York: Portfolio/Penguin, 2021.

Kluger, Avraham N., and Angelo DeNisi. "The Effects of Feedback Interventions on Performance: A Historical Review, a Meta-Analysis, and a Preliminary Feedback Intervention Theory." *Psychological Bulletin* 119, no. 2 (1996): 254-284. https://psycnet.apa.org/doiLanding?doi=10.1037%2F0033-2909.119.2.254.

Merriam-Webster. s.v. "feedback (*n.*)." Accessed August 23, 2021. https://www.merriam-webster.com/dictionary/feedback.

Solomon, Lou. "Two-Thirds of Managers Are Uncomfortable Communicating with Employees." *Harvard Business Review,* March 09, 2016. https://hbr.org/2016/03/two-thirds-of-managers-are-uncomfortable-communicating-with-employees.

Stone, Douglas, and Sheila Heen. *Thanks for the Feedback: The Science and Art of Receiving Feedback Well (Even When It Is off Base, Unfair, Poorly Delivered, and Frankly, You're Not in the Mood).* New York: Viking/Penguin, 2014.

Weber, Austin. "The Hawthorne Works." *Assembly,* August 1, 2002. https://www.assemblymag.com/articles/88188-the-hawthorne-works?v=preview.

Wigert, Ben, and Nate Dvorak. "Feedback Is Not Enough." *Gallup, Inc.,* May 16, 2019. https://www.gallup.com/workplace/257582/feedback-not-enough.aspx.

CHAPTER TWO: THE IMPACT OF BULLYING

Amaechi, John. "How to Build an Inclusive Workplace." Interviewed by Adam Grant. *Worklife with Adam Grant,* TED, April 20, 2021. Audio, 31:43. https://open.spotify.com/episode/13LAuqU4Pn2nCiAuM76qyL.

Appleton, Thomas. "Mr. Rogers and the Most Famous Defense of CPB Funding." *THIRTEEN — New York Public Media*, April 30, 2018. https://www.thirteen.org/blog-post/remembering-fred-rogers-defense-cpb/.

Dobkin, Lawrence, dir. *Star Trek: The Original Series.* Season 1, episode 2, "Charlie X." Aired September 15, 1969, on NBC. https://www.amazon.com/Mudds-Women/dp/B000HKYOKo/ref=sr_1_2?crid=JAW5YVK4Q1UZ&dchild=1&keywords=star+trek+the+original+series+season+1&qid=1630454847&s=instant-video&sprefix=Star+Trek+the+or%2Cinstant-video%2C166&sr=1-2.

Edwards, Gavin, and R. Sikoryak. *Kindness and Wonder: Why Mister Rogers Matters Now More Than Ever.* New York: Dey Street, an imprint of William Morrow, 2019.

Extension of Authorizations Under the Public Broadcasting Act of 1967 Hearings before the United States Senate Committee on Commerce, Subcommittee on Communications, Ninety-First Congress, First Session, Apr. 30, May 1, 1969. Washington: U.S. G.P.O., 1973.

Manson, Mark. *The Subtle Art of Not Giving a Fu*k: A Counterintuitive Approach to Living a Good Life.* New York: HarperOne, 2016.

Merriam-Webster. s.v. "feedback (*n.*)." Accessed August 23, 2021. https://www.merriam-webster.com/dictionary/feedback.

Namie, Gary. "Workplace Bullying: Escalated Incivility." *Ivey Business Journal* 68, no. 2 (2003): 1-6. https://www.rit.edu/~w-aaup/documents_not_rit/ivey_workplace_bulling.pdf.

Neville, Morgan, Caryn Capotosto, Nicholas Ma, Fred Rogers, Joanne Rogers, McColm Cephas, François Clemmons, et al. Won't You Be My Neighbor?. Widescreen. Universal City, CA: Universal Pictures Home Entertainment, 2018.

Salin, Denise. "Ways of Explaining Workplace Bullying: A Review of Enabling, Motivating and Precipitating Structures and Processes in the Work Environment." *Human Relations (New York)* 56, no. 10 (2003): 1213–32. https://doi.org/10.1177/00187267035610003.

Suggala, Susmita, Sujo Thomas, and Sonal Kureshi. "Impact of Workplace Bullying on Employees' Mental Health and Self-Worth." *The Palgrave Handbook of Workplace Well-Being* (2021): 799-818. https://www.researchgate.net/profile/Sujo-Thomas/publication/341426087_Impact_of_Workplace_Bullying_on_Employees%27_Mental_Health_and_Self-worth_-_The_Palgrave_Handbook_of_Workplace_Well-Being/links/5f8fdc1092851c14bcd86840/Impact-of-Workplace-Bullying-on-Employees-Mental-Health-and-Self-worth-The-Palgrave-Handbook-of-Workplace-Well-Being.pdf.

Van Heugten, Kate. "Resilience as an Underexplored Outcome of Workplace Bullying." *Qualitative Health Research* 23, no. 3 (2013): 291–301. https://doi.org/10.1177/1049732312468251.

Zak, Paul J. "The Neuroscience of Trust." *Harvard Business Review,* January–February 2017. https://hbr.org/2017/01/the-neuroscience-of-trust.

CHAPTER THREE: RESILIENT-BASED FEEDBACK

Boyatzis, Richard E., Kylie Rochford, and Scott N. Taylor. "The Role of the Positive Emotional Attractor in Vision and Shared Vision: Toward Effective Leadership, Relationships, and Engagement." *Frontiers in Psychology* 6 (2015): 670–670. https://doi. org/10.3389/fpsyg.2015.00670.

Boyatzis, Richard E., Melvin Smith, and Ellen Van Oosten. *Helping People Change: Coaching with Compassion for Lifelong Learning and Growth*. Boston, Massachusetts: Harvard Business Review Press, 2019.

Brown, Adrienne M. *Emergent Strategy: Shaping Change, Changing Worlds*. Chico, CA: AK Press, 2017.

Devonshire, Andy, dir. *The Great British Baking Show*. Season 1, episode 1, "Cake." Aired December 28, 2014, on PBS. https://www. pbs.org/food/features/great-british-baking-show-episodes/.

Merriam-Webster. s.v. "resilience (*n*.)." Accessed June 19, 2021. https://www.merriam-webster.com/dictionary/resilience.

Woods, David D. "Four Concepts for Resilience and the Implications for the Future of Resilience Engineering." *Reliability Engineering & System Safety* 141 (2015): 5–9. https://doi.org/10.1016/j. ress.2015.03.018.

CHAPTER FOUR: EXPANSIVE THINKING

Amabile, Teresa M., and Steven J. Kramer. "The Power of Small Wins." *Harvard Business Review,* May 2011. https://hbr.org/2011/05/ the-power-of-small-wins.

Bilalić, Merim, Peter McLeod, and Fernand Gobet. "Why Good Thoughts Block Better Ones: The Mechanism of the Pernicious Einstellung (set) Effect." *Cognition* 108, no. 3 (2008): 652–61. https:// doi.org/10.1016/j.cognition.2008.05.005.

Casad, B. J. "Confirmation bias." *Encyclopedia Britannica*, October 9, 2019. https://www.britannica.com/science/confirmation-bias.

Doldor, Elena, Madeleine Wyatt, and Jo Silvester. "Statesmen or Cheerleaders? Using Topic Modeling to Examine Gendered Messages in Narrative Developmental Feedback for Leaders." *The Leadership Quarterly* 30, no. 5 (2019): 101308–. https://doi.org/10.1016/j.leaqua.2019.101308.

Fey, Tina. *Bossypants*. New York: Little, Brown and Co., 2011.

Friedell, Nick. "Heat's Jimmy Butler Wants No Name on Back of Jersey." *ESPN*, July 14, 2020. https://www.espn.com.sg/nba/story/_/id/29461561/heat-jimmy-butler-wants-no-name-back-jersey.

Hirsch, Joe. *The Feedback Fix: Dump the Past, Embrace the Future, and Lead the Way to Change*. Lanham, Maryland: Rowman & Littlefield, 2017.

Hough, Karen. *The Improvisation Edge: Secrets to Building Trust and Radical Collaboration at Work*. San Francisco: Berrrett-Koehler Publishers, 2011.

Sisario, Ben. "Postal Service Tale: Indie Rock, Snail Mail and Trademark Law." *New York Times*, November 6, 2004. https://www.nytimes.com/2004/11/06/arts/music/postal-service-tale-indie-rock-snail-mail-and-trademark-law.html.

Spears, Marc J. "Source: NBA, Union Agree to List of Social Messages That Can Be Put On Jerseys." *ESPN*, July 3, 2020. https://www.espn.com/nba/story/_/id/29405787/source-nba-union-agree-list-social-messages-put-jerseys.

Stein, Marc (@TheSteinLine). "NBA spokesman on Jimmy Butler: "Displaying no name or message on the back of a player's jersey was not an option among the social justice messages agreed upon by the Players Association and the NBA as modifications to the rules regarding uniforms." Twitter, August 1, 2020. https://twitter.com/TheSteinLine/status/1289648908637880320?s=20.

CHAPTER FIVE: PERSISTENT CONVERSATION

Ali, Aisha J., Javier Fuenzalida, Margarita Gómez, and Martin J. Williams. "Four Lenses on People Management in the Public Sector: An Evidence Review and Synthesis." *Oxford Review of Economic Policy 37*, no. 2 (2021): 335–66. https://doi.org/10.1093/oxrep/grab003.

Bennett, Chris. "Running Easy Makes Hard Running Feel Way Easier—Here's How." *Runner's World*(blog). July 3, 2019. https://www.runnersworld.com/training/a28071070/how-to-make-running-easier/.

Gragnano, Andrea, Silvia Simbula, and Massimo Miglioretti. "Work-Life Balance: Weighing the Importance of Work-Family and Work-Health Balance." *International Journal of Environmental Research and Public Health 17*, no. 3 (2020): 907. https://doi.org/10.3390/ijerph17030907.

IDEO.org. "What is Human-Centered Design?" November 12, 2015. Video, 1:55. https://www.youtube.com/watch?v=musmgKEPY2o.

Rankin, Walter, and Jeremy Stanton. "Human-Centered Design in Higher Education." *Operations & Efficiency* (blog). *The EvoLLLution*, July 8, 2016. https://evolllution.com/managing-institution/operations_efficiency/human-centered-design-in-higher-education/.

99U. "Kat Holmes: Rethink What Inclusive Design Means." June 26, 2019. Video, 20:50. https://www.youtube.com/watch?v=-ic-cWRhKZa8.

Boyatzis, Richard E., Melvin Smith, and Ellen Van Oosten. *Helping People Change: Coaching with Compassion for Lifelong Learning and Growth*. Boston, Massachusetts: Harvard Business Review Press, 2019.

Brown, Brené. *Dare to Lead: Brave Work. Tough Conversations. Whole Hearts*. New York: Random House, 2018.

Gorney, Cynthia. "Curb Cuts." Interviewed by Delaney Hall. *99% Invisible*, April 27, 2021. Audio, 52:55. https://open.spotify.com/episode/2DKkoQiEsaco6MGiKY96P2.

Holmes, Kat. *Mismatch: How Inclusion Shapes Design*. Cambridge, MA: MIT Press, 2018.

Liston, Valerie. "Behind the Design: OXO's Iconic Good Grips Handles." *Good Tips* (blog). *OXO*, January 31, 2017. https://www.oxo.com/blog/behind-the-scenes/behind-design-oxos-iconic-good-grips-handles/.

Microsoft. "Inclusive: A Film about Innovative Design." June 28, 2016. Video, 21:10. https://news.microsoft.com/videos/inclusive/.

Sheridan, Emma. "The Curb Cut Effect: How Universal Design Makes Things Better for Everyone." (blog). *UX Collective*. February 2, 2021. https://uxdesign.cc/the-curb-cut-effect-universal-design-b4e3d7da73f5.

CHAPTER SEVEN: COMPASSIONATE LISTENING
Brown, Adrienne M. *Emergent Strategy: Shaping Change, Changing Worlds.* Chico, CA: AK Press, 2017.

Murphy, Kate. *You're Not Listening: What You're Missing and Why It Matters.* New York: Celadon Books, 2020.

Roy, Michael M., and Michael J. Liersch. "I Am a Better Driver Than You Think: Examining Self-Enhancement for Driving Ability." *Journal of Applied Social Psychology* 43, no. 8 (2013): 1648–59. https://doi.org/10.1111/jasp.12117.

Savitsky, Kenneth, Boaz Keysar, Nicholas Epley, Travis Carter, and Ashley Swanson. "The Closeness-Communication Bias: Increased Egocentrism Among Friends Versus Strangers." *Journal of Experimental Social Psychology* 47, no. 1 (2011): 269–73. https://doi.org/10.1016/j.jesp.2010.09.005.

CHAPTER EIGHT: STUDENTS & EARLY CAREER PROFESSIONALS
Brown, Adrienne M. *Emergent Strategy: Shaping Change, Changing Worlds.* Chico, CA: AK Press, 2017.

Clifton, Jim, and Jim Harter. *Wellbeing at Work.* New York: Gallup Press, 2021.

Fredrickson, Barbara L. "Updated Thinking on Positivity Ratios." *The American Psychologist* 68, no. 9 (2013): 814–22. https://doi.org/10.1037/a0033584.

Merriam-Webster. s.v. "*hyperextend* (v.)." Accessed June 19, 2021. https://www.merriam-webster.com/dictionary/hyperextend.

Philbrook, Amy. "Success in 2020 and Beyond: Curating a Roster of Confidants to Help You Soar." (blog). *LinkedIn,* January 30, 2020. https://www.linkedin.com/pulse/success-2020-beyond-curating-roster-confidants-help-amy/.

CHAPTER NINE: EDUCATORS & MANAGERS
Clifton, Jim, and Jim Harter. *Wellbeing at Work.* New York: Gallup Press, 2021.

Coutifaris, Constantinos GV, and Adam M. Grant. "Taking Your Team Behind the Curtain: The Effects of Leader Feedback-Sharing and Feedback-Seeking on Team Psychological Safety." *Organization Science* (2021). https://pubsonline.informs.org/doi/fpi/10.1287/orsc.2021.1498.

World Health Organization. "Burn-out an 'Occupational Phenomenon': International Classification of Diseases." World Health Organization. Press release, May 28, 2019. World Health Organization. website. https://www.who.int/news/item/28-05-2019-burn-out-an-occupational-phenomenon-international-classification-of-diseases, accessed June 19, 2021.